THE SURGE

The Leadership Network Innovation Series

LEADERSHIP ✦ NETWORK
innovation series

PETE BRISCOE

with TODD HILLARD

Churches *Catching the Wave*
of Christ's Love for the Nations

THE SURGE

ZONDERVAN

The Surge
Copyright © 2010 by Pete Briscoe

This title is also available as a Zondervan ebook. Visit www.zondervan.com/ebooks.

This title is also available in a Zondervan audio edition. Visit www.zondervan.fm.

Requests for information should be addressed to:

Zondervan, *Grand Rapids, Michigan* 49530

Library of Congress Cataloging-in-Publication Data

Briscoe, Pete, 1963 –
    The surge : churches catching the wave of Christ's love for the nations / Pete Briscoe with
Todd Hillard.
       p. cm.
    Includes bibliographical references.
    ISBN 978-0-310-28657-8 (softcover)
    1. Missions. 2. Church work. 3. Church renewal. 4. Mission of the church. I. Hillard, Todd,
1963 – II. Title.
BV2061.3.B75 2010
    262.001'7 – dc22
                                                     2010028325

Cover design: *Rob Monacelli*
Cover photography: *Ryan McVay/Getty Images*
Interior design: *Matthew VanZomeren*

Printed in the United States of America

10 11 12 13 14 15 /DCI/ 21 20 19 18 17 16 15 14 13 12 11 10 9 8 7 6 5 4 3 2 1

When the Surge arrived
at Bent Tree Bible Fellowship,
you got swept away.

You wept over the lost,
you grieved over injustice,
you prayed over the work,
you went over there,
you gave over and above.

To my siblings at Bent Tree,
I dedicate this book.
What a joy and privilege it is
to be your pastor, brother, and friend.
I love you.

CONTENTS

8. Go
9. Yes

ACKNOWLEDGMENTS

This book flows from within with passion, angst, and enthusiasm, but those feelings are not enough to produce a good book. A good book requires a good writer, a good editor, good content, and a publishing house that does all the detail work. This book was blessed with all of these things.

A Good Writer. Todd Hillard, who makes my passion sing in words.

A Good Editor. Ryan Pazdur, who helped shape the manuscript and then gave marvelous and critical input that vastly improved the final work. Thanks for making it better, Ryan!

Good Content. We have drawn on the writings and experiences of dozens of people, and those thoughts, ideas, and stories provided the backbone of this book. Among many others, we are grateful to Bruce Koch, David Bryant, Derrah Jackson, John Piper, Mike Neukum, Amy Cedrone, and the late Ralph Winter, who defined the mission for our generation.

A Good Publishing House. This book is a team effort with Zondervan and Leadership Network. I have been intimately involved with LN for almost twenty years now and see them as crucial partners in ministry. This is my first opportunity to work with the fine people at Zondervan, and I have found them to be bright, aware, and diligent.

Jesus, you are the substance of the Surge. You are everything. It is pure joy to offer this book to you to be used, as you see fit, for your purposes in the church.

SOMEWHERE IN THE DESERT OF WESTERN CHRISTIANITY

> As a father has compassion on his children, so the LORD has compassion on those who fear him; for he knows how we are formed, he remembers that we are dust. As for man, his days are like grass, he flourishes like a flower of the field; the wind blows over it and it is gone, and its place remembers it no more.
>
> — *Psalm 103:13 – 16*

Let's just say I'm very thankful that last year is in the rearview mirror. It was one of those years, the kind of year that you are thankful for in your mind, but only as a willful act of obedience, not as a heartfelt praise for all that went down. It began with so much promise. We were just putting the finishing touches on an expansion to our facility. Months and months of dirt and sawdust were settling, and I was flying high with both relief and expectations. (If you've been there, you know what I mean. Building projects both big and small can take their toll.)

But finally, that was all behind us. We were filling our new spaces with children and families and teaching and worship. The new staff offices were bright and open, fostering the interactive, creative atmosphere that I had always dreamed of. By numerical standards at least, Bent Tree Bible was already a success. We had missionaries on every continent (except Antarctica, still working on that one) and ministry spreading through the neighborhoods of north Dallas. And now we had more than doubled our square footage. I was pumped up, geared up, and ready to start looking outward again.

Then storm clouds began to billow. And unfortunately they weren't on the Texas skyline; they were within the leadership of our church. The winds of conflict hit us with a vengeance, the tension tearing apart relationships that we held so dear. I felt as though our body was being stabbed and dismembered from the inside out. More than once my wife, Libby, and I turned to each other and asked, "Is it worth it?" The question wasn't rhetorical. We sincerely didn't know. After years of growing together with Bent Tree Bible Fellowship, we were just about ready to call it quits, pack up our family, and walk away.

Physically, emotionally, and spiritually, we had found ourselves in the desert. Far from bringing us life-giving waters, our church experience had left us high and dry in a stinging storm of blowing sands. The good days were obscured by dust. The bad days left us blinded, unable to see at all. And it was taking its toll. Thirsty and tired, we were barely standing against the winds, staggering, doing our best just to survive.

Honest Questions in Dry Places

That's not just our story, is it? God loves his bride, but as servant leaders, our devotion to the church can inadvertently drain us, disillusion us, and even depress us. Over time, our calling can be slowly reduced to obligatory religious work; and institutional religion, true to its form, never fails to offer us a multitude of opportunities to work harder and harder. We have traditions to uphold, committees to administrate, and a merry-go-round of programs that spin our lives week to week, month to month, year to year without end, and *then* the storms come.

No question about it. It's tough to lead and difficult to innovate. But perhaps the hardest thing to face is that what we are doing doesn't seem to be working. According to the way we measure progress, things seem to be going in the wrong direction. Western Christianity, as a whole, is losing ground:

- According to the Barna Research Group, Christianity has grown at such a slow rate that Christians are not even winning their own children. While the population of the United States has grown by twenty-five million in the past fifteen years, church membership has declined by five million.

- In the book *Unchristian: What a New Generation Really Thinks about Christianity ... and Why It Matters*,[1] David Kinnaman's research shows that the unchurched generation of older mosaics and young busters (ages nineteen to thirty-two in 2010) have overwhelmingly negative views of Christians. In fact, only 10 percent of them had a "good impression" of born-again Christians, and only 3 percent had a "good impression" of evangelicals.

- Princeton's Dr. Robert Wuthrow, in a statistic-laden speech given October 4, 2007, claimed that "there has actually been a slow but definite long-term slide in churchgoing of about a quarter of a percentage point each year. Overall, between 5 percent and 6 percent fewer Americans participate regularly in religious services now than in the early 70s, so that is a loss, conservatively, of ten million regular churchgoers."

- The April 13, 2009, *Newsweek* cover story proclaimed "The End of Christian America." The survey which spawned the article, the 2009 American Religious Identification Survey, made it clear that "the percentage of self-identified Christians has fallen 10 percentage points since 1990, from 86 to 76 percent."

The numbers don't paint a pretty picture, and most of us are right in the middle of that picture. Sure, there are pockets of enthusiasm and encouragement. Some local congregations continue to see tremendous numerical and spiritual growth. Undoubtedly, we see regular victory in individual souls as the Holy Spirit faithfully and continually draws Westerners to himself. There is great rejoicing — as there should be — over the one sheep that was lost and becomes found. But a defeatist, defensive cloud has descended upon Western Christianity as a whole. Many of the leaders who are giving their all for the church feel like benchwarmers on the losing team in a game that no one even wants to play anymore. The church in the Western world has more resources, more money, and more means to minister than anyone else in the history of the church. Yet this elusive thing we call revival is now something from centuries past that Americans only read about. Where *is* the God of Elijah?

Meanwhile, our heads and hearts are continually turned by the latest and greatest strategies. We read the trendiest books, scan the hottest blogs, and sit expectantly in auditoriums with our conference notebooks open and pens ready, listening intently to those whose churches defy the statistics. Excitement and expectation rise, and we head for home with a dozen or more new ideal ways to do this thing we call ministry. Yet back home, we're left with the familiar sense of aloneness, beleaguered now with visions of things that we are not. Our souls stumble under the heavy weight of a new "to do" list. *If only I did ... If I just ... then would God begin to pour out the flood of his Spirit on this dusty land? Would the flywheel start to roll?*

In the hardest of times, in moments of quiet honesty, questions rise to the surface — genuine questions, often secret questions, spoken only to ourselves, lest we be forced to allow others to see the desperate search in our tired, doubtful eyes:

- What am I to be about? What am I *really* supposed to be doing? Please don't point me toward a meeting or a committee or repeat the lofty terms of some dusty vision statement. I'm too tired to play that game anymore.
- Who am I? Who am I *really*? Please don't define me by how I look or what I say or where you find me standing on any given Sunday morning or Wednesday night. I may have lost track of who I am, but at least I know I am deeper than what I do.

- And what about these people with whom I share the journey, this thing called church? Who are these people that I lead? Who are these people that I follow? Who are those who walk beside me as my friends, comrades, and partners in this peculiar faith? And to what have we been called, *really*?
- And ultimately: Does it matter? Does it *really* matter?

Doesn't a little nagging voice inside us ask that last question again and again? *Does it really matter? Is it really worth it?* Those are the questions Libby and I were facing when we found ourselves in the desert. Who hasn't, in the secret corners of their mind, echoed the exasperated sentiments of Solomon: "Everything is meaningless. All go to the same place; all come from dust, and to dust all return" (Eccl. 3:19 – 20)?

When the lights go out and we're staring at the ceiling waiting for sleep, who hasn't taken an inventory of their lives and ministries and questioned whether they are on the right track? What leader hasn't looked into the darkness and wondered if they haven't overlooked some vital variable in the equation of spiritual success, that missing variable that makes our heartfelt faith and the dusty realities of life mesh perfectly?

Out of the Desert

If you are all too familiar with this metaphorical desert, I'd like to invite you to listen with me, pray, and then walk with me out of the dry and dusty sands. We don't have to stay where we are. In the chapters ahead, our destination is a biblical paradigm for ministry and self-evaluation, a timeless matrix for innovative leadership, and a proven series of ideas for global networking. Some of the concepts will sound like echoes of words you have heard before, words like *missions* and *Great Commission* (which, I might add, don't appear in Scripture). I'll be avoiding terms like that — not because we aren't part of the great history of God's work across the globe but because what he is doing today is different from what we used to mean by those words. To get out of the desert of traditional thinking, we need a fresh envisioning of the unchanging purposes of God, a vision that feels like a cool, refreshing drink of living water for the soul of the thirsty leader.

Part 1 investigates

- the deluge of God's passion and the flood of his Spirit, which *is* being poured out on this world, creating a tsunami of praise across the globe;
- the central theme of redeeming "the nations" from Genesis to Revelation that gives the church universal a clear biblical measurement for success on the local church level, and how God is being unquestionably successful in this endeavor;
- why God's passion for each of us, as individual leaders, is a prerequisite for authentic Christian leadership.

Part 2 explores

- transforming technologies that are redefining global ministry;
- demographic shifts that are bringing the world to our own neighborhoods;
- faith, freedom, and finances in an earthly and heavenly perspective;
- how short-term experiences can make lifelong changes in you and your congregation;
- what happens when the Spirit of the sending God lives within us;
- how we, as adoptive children of God, can adopt entire nations in his name;
- why this really does matter, now and in eternity.

For the sake of your soul and the strength of your local church, I'm inviting you to submerge yourself in the rushing waters of God's global passion. I'm challenging you to stop right where you are, wherever you are in the desert, and listen for the distant thunder of life-giving rivers. I pray that in the pages ahead, you will begin to hear them and even feel them, and then turn your back on the desert interior and walk toward a new horizon, where the distant rumble becomes a deafening roar and you finally get to the shore of a new focus for life and ministry. Let the cool mist engulf you as you ponder the raging current of God's infinite, eternal passion for the world, for the nations ... and for you too.

Prepare to be swept away.

> The journey from the desert into the Surge is a very personal one. Share your story and read about others' stories in the forums at *www.GetInTheSurge.com*.

Part One

FROM DUST

You are but dust and to
dust you will return.
— Genesis 3:19

Chapter One

The Surge

God's Global Passion Unleashed

Surge (surj) noun. A sudden growth in size and intensity; a movement that increases in a billowing or swelling manner, as if in a wave.

Deserts are a reality on this planet, dry places devoid of the water that is essential for life. And sadly, we also find those places in our souls. Throughout Scripture, God uses dry places and dry times to shape the leaders he is preparing to use. Moses, Jesus, Paul — all go through their own versions of exile in dusty places. Is it possible that this is where he has brought his bride in the Western world? Today Western Christianity appears to be in a desert. In our hearts, it feels as though we have resigned ourselves to being on the defensive, struggling for survival as the world, the flesh, and the devil advance.

But nothing could be farther from the truth. To borrow from C. S. Lewis, "Aslan is on the move." The long winter is thawing, spring is upon us, and we are already seeing a harvest that is unprecedented since the first century.

We call it *the Surge*.

What is the Surge? The Surge is the global movement of our Savior's love, redeeming individuals and entire nations for the fulfillment of God's eternal purposes. The Surge is the accelerating completion of Matthew 24:14: "This gospel of the kingdom will be preached in the whole world as a testimony to all nations." It's Acts 1:8 in action as the Holy Spirit speaks his truth "to the ends of the earth." And it's the prelude to the uproar of worship John heard unleashed in Revelation 19: "I heard what sounded like the roar of a great multitude in heaven shouting: ... 'Hallelujah! For our Lord God Almighty reigns. Let us rejoice and be glad and give him glory!'" (vv. 1, 6 – 7).

Today the Surge is the visible sign of what God is doing to redeem this world through the love of Christ. We have read of it in history. We have experienced it in our souls. Now it is being unleashed across the globe.

Snapshots of the Surge

The Surge is visible in the lives of individuals. Several years ago, I met a young pastor in India who was reaching out to a large number of street people living under a village bridge on the Ganges River. The only way for this pastor to reach the people under the bridge was to climb down a forty-foot rope. One evening while climbing back up, his hands slipped and he fell the full forty feet. Six hours on an ox cart later, he arrived at the hospital, paralyzed from the neck down. As word spread, hundreds began praying. Two days later, he walked out of the hospital stiff and unable to bend down. Despite this painful limitation, he returned to the village where he had fallen.

In the same area, a powerful Hindu extremist had been pulling pastors out of their churches during their sermons and beating them, his hatred for Christians flowing through his fists. He was greatly feared, yet this young pastor sensed the Spirit prompting him to go to this man and share the gospel. Deathly afraid and still recovering from his fall, he followed God's lead. The Hindu man went berserk, and the young pastor ran from the house. But the Hindu holy man could not get the seed of the gospel out of his mind. He lost sleep — in fact, he couldn't sleep at all. After four months of being tormented by the truth, he prayed, "Jesus, if you are real, reveal yourself to me or I will end my life!" That night, at 4:00 a.m., a man appeared to him at the foot of the bed. "I am Jesus," he said. The next morning, the man was no longer a Hindu priest but a new creature in Christ. He is now a leader in the little church, making inroads in dark places.

The Surge is also flooding entire cities. In Cali, Columbia, during the 1980s, a ruthless drug cartel dominated the city, moving hundreds of millions of dollars' worth of cocaine in any given month and leaving in its wake a bloody war zone of fear and treachery. Isolated and segregated, pastors kept to themselves as their floundering congregations kept their heads low and tried to survive on streets heavy with spiritual oppression and physical danger. The drug cartel, it turned out, was deeply involved in the occult, adding witchcraft to its arsenal of weapons, drugs, and death.

Soon, however, God moved in the hearts of a few missionaries and pastors, who confessed their independent, separatist attitudes. Together they prayed aggressively against the spiritual and physical strongholds that imprisoned their city. God began to move, and the movement began to grow and grow and grow. Soon sixty thousand believers from across all denominations gathered for all-night prayer vigils in the city stadium. The next weekend, for the first time in several decades, no murders were reported. Within weeks, the leadership of the drug cartels began to crumble. Then one of the pastors was murdered, but his martyrdom only fueled the flames of revival. People by the thousands professed faith in Jesus, including key media figures and top city officials. In a relatively short time, the entire community was transformed. Children and families walk the streets in relative safety; places of worship are packed and overflowing. "God himself is moving in our city," proclaimed one sportscaster. "This is even more significant than soccer!" (And if you know anything about South America, you know that nothing is more significant than soccer.)

Even entire countries are feeling the rush of the Surge. In *Operation World, 21st Century Edition*, Patrick Johnstone and Jason Mandryk chronicle what God is doing country by country across the globe. (This book is an indispensable reference for anyone who wants at their fingertips key demographic information about every country — a highly recommended resource for intelligent prayer too.)

We are seeing strength and growth in many countries where state-sanctioned persecution is the norm, including Sudan, North Korea, India, China, and Ethiopia. Many countries, such as Turkey, were considered impenetrable only a few decades ago. They are proving to be fertile ground as the gospel is proclaimed with a pioneering spirit. Togo, a small country of 5 million on the Atlantic coast of Africa, has seen its population of evangelicals grow from 17,000 to nearly 400,000 between 1960 and 2000. The Assemblies of God had set a goal of 300 churches and 36,000 members by 2000 in Togo; at the end of that year, they could count more than 110,000 members.

Even continents are experiencing the power of the Surge.

Unparalleled harvests are taking place across the continents of Latin America, Asia, and Africa, causing a massive shift of Christianity's center of gravity to the non-Western world.

Comparison of Western and Non-Western Christians

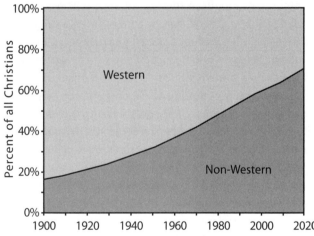

Taken from Patrick Johnstone and Jason Mandryk, *Operation World: 21st Century Edition* (Waynesboro, Ga.: Paternoster, 2001), 4.

That is incredible news, actually. While institutional Christianity declines in Europe and appears to be stagnating in North America and the Pacific, the Surge is on in many other parts of the globe. When we look at the whole world, God is moving, God is healing, God is redeeming in unprecedented ways. And it's happening today.

> Evangelical growth in Latin America in the twentieth century was spectacular. From 1900 to 2000, evangelicals grew from about 700,000 in number to over 55 million.
>
> — Jason Mandryk, coauthor of *Operation World*

None of us would deny, on a theological level, that God is at work in the world — "out there, somewhere" — but besides a few missionary stories, it all seems so distant. So much of what we are hearing is so far from our experience that we have a hard time believing it in our heads, let alone our hearts. As credible witnesses are documenting more and more accounts of the Surge around the globe, those of us in the desert are left wondering why we appear to have been left out.

> Christianity is now truly a global religion once more — a status it lost twelve centuries ago.
>
> — Patrick Johnstone and Jason Mandryk, *Operation World, 21st Century Edition*

Are we missing something? Do we need a new formula for evangelism? A new prayer mantra that will unleash the blessings of heaven?

I propose that getting into the Surge requires something more fundamental than that. It must begin with a mindset change — a surrendered heart — that transforms our lives and our ministry, even changing the way we interpret familiar passages of Scripture.

Stone Temples and Fig Trees

Several years ago, I was preparing a sermon on Mark 11 and came across a passage that had long perplexed me: "On reaching Jerusalem, Jesus entered the temple area and began driving out those who were buying and selling there. He overturned the tables of the money changers and the benches of those selling doves, and would not allow anyone to carry merchandise through the temple courts. And as he taught them, he said, 'Is it not written: "My house will be called a house of prayer for all nations"? But you have made it "a den of robbers"'" (Mark 11:15 – 17).

This account is often used to dissuade people from selling cookies in the church foyer, but I knew that there was more to this passage than what I was seeing. I decided to back up a bit and look at the passage in light of its historical and biblical contexts. I went all the way back to the beginning — to Genesis 1. In Eden, the first man and woman experienced a perfection that we simply cannot imagine. But it was not to last. There was a lie, there was a temptation, and choices were made from which we have never recovered. Still, God longed to be with his created. So God initiated a remarkable plan to reinstitute fellowship with his lost creatures. In the Old Testament, the Lord set up a simple system: *Build a big building, I'll live in it, and then people can come to spend time with me.* The scope of his intent was made clear in Isaiah 56:3 – 7, which Jesus quoted in Mark: "Let no foreigner who has bound himself to the Lord say, 'The Lord will surely exclude me from his people.' … And foreigners who bind themselves to the Lord to serve him, to love the name of the Lord, and to worship him, all who keep the Sabbath without desecrating it and who hold fast to my covenant — these I will bring to my holy mountain and give them joy in my house of prayer. Their burnt offerings and sacrifices will be accepted on my altar; for my house will be *called a house of prayer for all nations*" (Isa. 56:3 – 7, emphasis added).

I found this passage stunning. God intended that *all* people could come within the walls of the temple to find him. He intended to be accessible to all cultural groups and those from every stratum of society. His desire was that the whole world would be drawn to him to pray together!

Soon enough this all changed, however. An "us versus them" attitude emerged, and the Jewish religious establishment made the temple off-limits to the very people the Father wanted to see worshiping there. Gentiles could not enter the temple proper; a wall surrounding the sanctuary had signs cautioning Gentiles to stay in their designated area outside the walls. In fact, archaeologists have excavated two tablets that say, "No foreigner is to enter within the forecourt around the sanctuary. Whoever is caught will have himself to blame for his subsequent death."

That's part of the historical context of Mark 11, where we find Jesus, whip in hand, yelling at the authorities and turning over tables. Something amazing took place at the temple that day. But what was it?

Sacrifices Interrupted

As I grappled with this passage, for the first time I saw the divine purpose behind Jesus' actions. First, it is clear that Jesus intended to interrupt the sacrifice, and he did it with a purpose. Nothing in Mark 11:15 – 16 suggests that Jesus was angry over dishonest business practices. Notice that he threw out both the buyers and the sellers! Jesus did, however, cut off the cash flow that funded the daily sacrifices. The tables he overturned were set up to receive the annual half-shekel tax prescribed in Exodus 30, which required every Jewish male to fund the daily sacrifices. He also interfered with the selling of doves, doves that were the designated sacrifice for the purification of the poor, the women, and the cleansed lepers. Furthermore, he intercepted the worshipers "and would not allow anyone to carry merchandise through the temple courts." (The word translated "merchandise" is *skueos*, which refers to sacred temple vessels used in the rituals of worship.) Jesus interrupted the sacrifice because he would soon become the ultimate sacrifice.

Jacob Neusner said it this way: "Only someone who rejected the Torah's explicit teaching concerning the daily whole offering would have overturned the tables, or … someone who had in mind setting up a different table, for a different purpose."[2]

During the age of the old covenant, the temple represented a central location where all humankind could have access to God. That purpose had been seriously violated by the religious establishment. When Jesus breathed his last breath on the cross and the curtain of the temple was torn in two, one can almost picture the massive hands of God holding it between his thumbs and index fingers and tearing it while he proclaims, *Finally, now* all *can have access to me!*

Righteous Anger

Second, Jesus' actions clearly reflected his anger over the Jews' disobedience to the prophecy in Isaiah and the temple's purpose. He said, "Is it not written: 'My house will be called a house of prayer for all nations'?" Jesus was angered by the exclusivity of the Jewish leaders. The temple in Jerusalem had not become a place for all nations; it had become the centerpiece of the Jewish nation.

Usually when we arrive at this portion of the passage, we preach about the need for prayer in the church. (As one of my seminary professors once said to me after I preached a sermon for him, "Great sermon; wrong text!") Of course we need to pray in the church, and there are wonderful passages in the Bible that point us to that directive, but this is not one of them. The emphasis of this verse is not on "house of prayer"; it is on the phrase "for all nations." There are a handful of places in the Old Testament where the temple is called a house of prayer, but only one where "for all nations" is attached, and that's the passage in Isaiah that Jesus quoted.

Jesus' anger was not limited to the exclusivity of the Jewish leaders; it was stoked by their hypocrisy as well. The Jewish leaders were living wretched lifestyles, thinking one act of worship would make them okay with God and at the same time preventing the humble in heart from having access to God. They were using the temple as home base, assuming that as long as they gave sacrifices, God didn't really care what their Sunday through Friday looked like.

When Jesus said that they had turned the temple into "a den of robbers," he was quoting a scalding prophetic word given by Jeremiah at the gate of the temple. The religious elite were rebuked for "oppress[ing] the alien, the fatherless [and] the widow." Through Jeremiah, God asked them, "Will you steal and murder, commit adultery and perjury ... and then come and stand before me in this house, which bears my Name, and say, 'We are safe' — safe to do all these detestable things? Has this house, which bears my Name, become a den of robbers to you?" (Jer. 7:1 – 11).

The temple had become a religious cloak for evil in Jeremiah's day; Jesus was saying that the same treachery was taking place before him, and he was calling their bluff. It's no wonder they got so angry. The treachery against God's purpose for the temple was being exposed by this renegade itinerant preacher.

Ineffective and Irrelevant

Third, Jesus' actions showed how the temple in its current state had become ineffective and would soon, after Pentecost, become irrelevant. After Jesus rose from the dead and ascended to the Father, the Spirit of God began indwelling believers at Pentecost.[3] This truth — that the very Spirit of God now dwells in our lives — is not lofty theology but a mysterious and profoundly powerful reality. Jesus disqualified the old stone temple because he was about to create millions of human temples and send them out into the world to take himself to the masses. Our hearts are the temple of the Holy Spirit. They are the center stage where Jesus will act out his purposes in our times.

Once, during a summer sabbatical, I had the chance to travel in the Holy Land. We were able to make our way through the tunnel that goes under the Wailing Wall near the Temple Mount foundation in Jerusalem. Several Jewish synagogues have been built down there during the past ten years. At one of the synagogues, a group of women was praying reverently, their faces against the wall. This spot is as close as they can get to where the Holy of Holies likely existed when the temple stood. It's amazing to see how fervently they pray, so near where God's presence once dwelt, diligently asking God to turn this barren ground into a place of worship and sacrifice once more. But what is even more amazing is that we, as Christians, don't have to find a place to get close to God's presence. Since Pentecost, we are able to experience him in moment-by-moment intimacy because of his indwelling Spirit. I was astonished by the contrast. Women praying before dead rocks, yearning for the restoration of the temple, while we stood nearby with God's presence within us as his temples.

God had intended to use the temple as a place to draw the people of the world to himself. Now he was going to spread his blessings outward through individuals and the church!

It is no coincidence that Jesus' rampage in the temple took place between two significant events at a barren fig tree: "The next day as they were leaving Bethany, Jesus was hungry. Seeing in the distance a fig tree in leaf, he went to find out if it had any fruit. When he reached it, he found nothing but leaves, because it was not the season for figs. Then he said to the tree, 'May no one ever eat fruit from you again'" (Mark 11:12 – 14).

This seems a rather strange episode in Jesus' life. But understood in the context of Jesus' actions in the temple, the story of the fig tree gives us a metaphor to characterize the state of God's people at this time. Jesus found a temple that was "fruitless," much like the fig tree — a temple that had failed to fulfill its purposes — and he declared that no one would ever eat fruit from it again. Mark tells us that, the morning after Jesus cleared out the temple, the disciples saw the cursed tree once again. It was now withered. Upon seeing the withered tree, Jesus exhorted his disciples to have great faith in God, to expect great things through sincere prayer, and to live genuine lives of forgiveness. He knew that everything they knew and understood about God was about to change.

Instead of the "bring people to me at the building" strategy, Jesus implemented a radically different strategy: *My Spirit is now in you; take me to the people.*

And they did.

After Pentecost, the Surge began in full force. The global movement of the Savior's love, redeeming individuals and entire nations for the fulfillment of God's eternal purposes, was unleashed through a few followers of Jesus in an upper room near the temple. From this tiny band of Jewish believers, the church spread throughout most of the Roman Empire at an exponential rate. Historians estimate that the entire known world probably was reached with the news of this sacrificial Savior within a few decades.

But then somebody built a building.

We can probably blame this on Constantine. As Roman emperor, in the early 300s he declared Christianity to be an official religion. He began sanctioning the building of buildings to house this newly formed religious institution. I'm not sure that we have ever recovered from this. Before Constantine, "church" consisted of nothing more (and nothing less) than an ever-expanding network of human beings indwelt by the Holy Spirit of God himself. Now the dictionary defines *church* as "a building for public Christian worship." That's not just a semantic shift. We are stuck with an artificial and obstructive paradigm, and I'm afraid that this concept, as well as the buildings themselves, is obscuring our primary purpose — to find our place in the current of God's passion for the nations.

Rethinking the Assumed

Let me ask you an honest (but dangerously leading) question: is it too much to say that we've returned to the temple strategy of the Old Testament? Rather than taking Jesus to the world, are not most of us primarily consumed with trying to get people to come to a building? Let's be honest. Haven't we been obsessed with the news that fewer people than ever are stepping into a building for two hours on a Sunday morning? Isn't this what drives our concerns?

Is it possible that the stagnation of Western evangelicalism is not itself the problem but rather a symptom of this archaic strategy? Have we become so enamored with our meetings and our buildings and our programs that we have become consumed with ourselves?

I say it's time to bust out of the temple strategy again. It's time to find answers to the hard questions plaguing us. It's time to examine our assumptions about ourselves, our ministries, and our churches. It's time to get caught up in the Surge, but to do this, we must first learn to see the world with new eyes.

The Surge is a global movement in which every member of the body of Christ matters. Share your thoughts, voice your opinions, contribute your resources, and tell about your experiences at *www.GetInTheSurge.com*.

Chapter Two

Defining Moments

God's Vision for the Nations

> Nothing is as powerful as an idea whose time has come.
> Armies can be resisted; but not an idea whose time has come.
> — *Victor Hugo*

Every month, the Willow Creek *Defining Moments* CD arrives in my mail slot to remind me of important defining moments I've had as a pastor:

1. *Defining Moment 1:* There was the time I heard Jim Dethmer talk with astounding vulnerability. I learned from Jim that sharing weakness is life-giving to the listener.
2. *Defining Moment 2:* Bill Hybels and Nancy Beach discussed Willow's train wreck with startling honesty, and I learned that sharing your failures does not diminish your credibility; it increases it.
3. *Defining Moment 3:* I fell in love with preaching again when John Ortberg magnificently described the joy and privilege of the craft.

The greatest defining moment for me, however, was a statement Bill Hybels made in an early Leadership Summit: "I believe the church is the hope of the world, and her effectiveness lies primarily in her leadership." As I sat in the audience, I disagreed with Bill in my mind and started to scribble my arguments on my conference notebook. I had two fundamental problems with the statement:

1. The church is not the hope of the world; Christ is.
2. The church's effectiveness lies primarily in the power of the Holy Spirit, not in her leaders.

After arguing with Bill on my pad, I wrote out a statement that I truly believe: "I am convinced that Christ is the hope of a dying, desperate, and deluded world. Because the church carries with her the life, love, and message of Christ, the church delivers that hope."

As I sat in the far reaches of the balcony, the rest of the conference participants disappeared around me. I was all alone. I read my statement over and over again and found my pulse racing and my heart bursting with anticipation. *Yes!* I thought. *This is why the church is so important; this is why I love her so!* It was a defining moment for me and our church.

Today our mission statement reads, "Bent Tree exists to be used by God as he transforms people into disciples of Jesus Christ, here and around the world." When we rewrote it recently, we added the "here and around the world" part at the end. It's not just a motto for us; it's our daily mission.

Willow Creek reminded the church that the lost are all around us, Saddleback taught us that the found need to be developed, North Point has pointed out that multisite churches can reach scores of people, and the Emerging Church has called us all to deep, sacrificial, and authentic missional living in our community. At Bent Tree, we have learned from these innovative churches and movements. Our humble prayer is that we would be used by God in some way to remind the church of "the rest of the world" — the nations and people groups that lack a witness to the gospel of God's grace.

God has taken us on a journey, and in many ways we are still in the early stages of it. Technology and methodology are continually morphing us into something different, but one thing never changes, and that is the biblical foundation of the Surge. The grass withers and the flowers fade, but the Word of God stands forever, and God's Word, from beginning to end, speaks of his passion and purpose for the nations.

The Great Paradigm Shift

The word *nation* doesn't quite mean what it used to mean. Like many words, *nation* has taken on a different definition in our contemporary world dominated by politics. The Greek word for nation is *ethne*, the same root we use for the English word *ethnic*. We still use the word *nation* in this sense in phrases such as the "Cherokee Nation," or even when we talk about Hitler's "Arian Nation," to distinguish between groups of people along ethnic and cultural lines rather than just political ones. Missiologists often refer to these ethnically distinguished nations as "people groups." The Lausanne Committee on World Evangelization defined a people group this way: "the largest group within which the Gospel can spread as a church planting movement without encountering barriers of understanding or acceptance" (1982 Lausanne Committee Chicago meeting). Anthropologists and ethnographers calculate that there are approximately twenty-four thousand distinguishable people groups dispersed among the 220 or so political nations.[4]

Why is this important? The word for people groups, *ethnos*, is the same word that Jesus used in Matthew 28 when he commanded his ragtag band of followers to "go and make disciples of all nations." Most of us seem to have a pretty good understanding of the "make disciples" mandate of this verse, but what about "all nations"? Was this an afterthought that Jesus threw out there at the end?

Hardly. God's passion for all nations can be found in Genesis and Revelation and everywhere in between, though looking for it is a little bit like trying to see individual trees in a forest. Still, if you look for this theme — or even just do a simple search for the words *the nations* and *the peoples* and *the whole earth* — suddenly God's intention and God's heart for the entire world start showing up on page after page. Here is a quick (and by no means comprehensive) sample from the Old Testament:

- *Genesis 12:3.* God blessed Abraham so that "all peoples on earth will be blessed through you."
- *Deuteronomy 28:9 – 10.* "The LORD will establish you [Israel] as his holy people.... Then all the peoples on earth will see that you are called by the name of the LORD."
- *1 Samuel 17:46.* What was David's passion when he squared off with Goliath? "This day the LORD will hand you over to me, and I'll strike you down and cut off your head.... And the whole world will know that there is a God in Israel."
- *1 Chronicles 16:23 – 24.* When the ark was returned to Jerusalem, David proclaimed, "Sing to the LORD, all the earth.... Declare his glory among the nations, his marvelous deeds among all peoples."
- *2 Chronicles 6:32 – 33.* We see again God's intent for the temple. "As for the foreigner who does not belong to your people Israel ... when he comes and prays toward this temple ... do whatever the foreigner asks of you, so that all the peoples of the earth may know your name."
- *Psalm 108:3.* Old Testament worship lyrics are filled with this theme. "I will praise you, O LORD, among the nations; I will sing of you among the peoples."
- *Isaiah 49:6.* God proclaimed to the exiled of Israel that "I will also make you a light for the Gentiles, that you may bring my salvation to the ends of the earth."
- *Jeremiah 33:9.* When God promised to restore the communities destroyed by the Babylonian invasion, he proclaimed, "Then this city will bring me renown, joy, praise

and honor before all nations on earth that hear of all the good things I do for it."

- *Daniel 7:13 – 14.* In one of Daniel's visions, he saw that "there before me was one like a son of man.... He was given authority, glory and sovereign power; all peoples, nations and men of every language worshiped him."
- *Malachi 1:11.* In the last book of the Old Testament, the Lord Almighty proclaimed, "My name will be great among the nations, from the rising to the setting of the sun. In every place incense and pure offerings will be brought to my name, because my name will be great among the nations."
- Among dozens of other passages, see also 2 Sam. 22:50; Ps. 150:6; Mic. 4:3; Nah. 1:5; Hab. 2:14; Zec. 14:9.

The Great Commission was not simply a postscript to the main text of the Old Testament. Christ was restating what God's priorities have always been. At the risk of overkill, let's take a look at a handful of New Testament passages as well:

- *Mark 13:10.* "The gospel must first be preached to all nations."
- *Luke 24:47.* "Repentance and forgiveness of sins will be preached in his name to all nations, beginning at Jerusalem."
- *Romans 1:5.* "We received grace and apostleship to call people from among all the Gentiles."
- *Galatians 3:14.* "... that in Christ Jesus the blessing of Abraham might come upon the Gentiles, that we might receive the promise of the Spirit through faith" (RSV).
- *Philippians 2:10 – 11.* "... that at the name of Jesus every knee should bow, in heaven and on earth ... and every tongue confess that Jesus Christ is Lord."
- See also John 10:16; 1 Cor. 15:24; 2 Cor. 5:19; Eph. 1:10; 1 Thess. 1:8; 1 Tim. 3:16; 1 John 4:14; 3 John 6 – 7.

David Bryant, in the groundbreaking book *In the Gap*, traced God's passion for the nations through every book of the Bible. And in his book *Unveiled at Last*, Bob Sjogren lists more than five hundred passages that reveal God's concern for the nations! God's heart is focused like a laser beam on the nations, these individual pockets of twenty-four thousand peoples that make up the world that he loves so much that he gave his only Son to die for. It's God's strategic passion that every person on earth have an opportunity to hear about him in a language they can understand in a context that makes sense in their culture; it's his plan that the good news of hope be expressed by disciples who have been made within each people group.

> Christians can escape the sorcery of self-centeredness. Like a mighty wind the Spirit of God can reverse the introverted patterns in our discipleship. He can uncover for us a crystal view of God's majestic horizons — Christ's global cause.... God's Holy Wind can free us to move out, breathing deeply and seeing clearly ... released to be all we were meant to be. Free to be World Christians.
>
> — David Bryant, *In the Gap*

One verse about the nations should be enough to lead us, as Bible believers, into prayerful response. The overwhelming emphasis God places on the nations in Scripture should cause us to reconsider the paradigm of our faith. The Surge — God's passionate love for the nations — is not just to be compartmentalized away in a mission committee. It's a central theme that permeates everything we as the church are and will be until Jesus returns.

I realize that most of us are already heavily invested in programs and initiatives — many of them good and effective ministries to our communities — that take much of our time and energy. And a shift in our focus will likely necessitate a change in our priorities. If you are like me (and like most pastors and church leaders I know), some familiar concerns may be speaking quite loudly to you right now, some initial objections to what I am saying.

- *Objection 1*: This isn't me. I'm not called to this stuff.
- *Objection 2*: Wouldn't this mean neglecting our neighbors?
- *Objection 3*: Wouldn't this be done at the expense of the local church?

I suggest that these are the wrong questions to be asking. Instead we need to take a step back from our contexts and consider the bigger picture. We need to consider what the consequences likely will be if we continue to neglect our purpose as a church. Can we continue to ignore God's passion for the nations and unreached people of the world without becoming just another example of the self-indulgent Western church?

This is not a rhetorical question. Why does Western Christianity seem to be mired in the pool of its own stagnation? Why are so many of its leaders tired, burned out, and disillusioned? Some suggest that the problem is that our forms of worship are archaic. Others tell us that we have lost our passion for preaching the Word. Or they point to the evidence that our culture has become oppressively secular.

There might be some truth in each of these, but let me suggest another possibility: What if the real cause of our struggles in the Western church is that we have lost continuity with our fundamental design? If we consider that Scripture repeatedly testifies to God's passion for the nations, how is it that our contemporary evangelical churches continue to allocate ridiculously small percentages of our efforts and resources to this cause? If God's passion for the nations permeates human history, why is it that many of our congregations have delegated this responsibility to a committee run by a few individuals?

We are largely fixated on a "come to the building" temple strategy that excludes the nations. This was not simply a problem in Jesus' time; it is alive and well in contemporary evangelicalism! Our focus on buildings and the size of our congregations skews our worldview and even shapes our hermeneutic.

As an example of what I'm saying, let's take a quick look at one of the most common texts churches use to define their approach to missions: "When they met together, they asked him, 'Lord, are you at this time going to restore the kingdom to Israel?' He said to them: 'It is not for you to know the times or dates the Father has set by his own authority. But you will receive power when the Holy Spirit comes on you; and you will be my witnesses in Jerusalem, and in all Judea and Samaria, and to the ends of the earth'" (Acts 1:6–8).

The disciples were still operating under the impression that Jesus was going to build his kingdom by restoring a central place of worship for all. But Jesus had something different in mind for his followers. He said to them, *You will be the ones who will take the kingdom to the world, boys! Here is the game plan: Start close to home (Jerusalem) and reach out to the lost around you. Then expand your reach to the outskirts of your area (Judea) so that more may know the truth. Then lean into those who live near you but are ethnically different from you (Samaria), because they desperately need the message as well. And after you are being used in increasing ways, stretch out your hands in grace to the far reaches of the earth (the ends of the world) and don't stop until you have gotten into every nook and cranny of humankind, because I want everyone to have access to my Father!*

Now, if you were to take a look at how most churches use this verse today, it would go something like this: Every local church should first reach "Jerusalem" (their own city). Then they should reach their own "Judea/Samaria" (their region, state, or country). Then, if there's any money or energy remaining (which is rare), the church should try to reach for the ends of the earth.

There are a couple of problems with this way of applying the passage. First, there is the problem of priority. If we are honest, we know that our tendency is to become so consumed with our "Jerusalem" projects and programs that we rarely make it to "Judea/

Samaria" and almost never have time or resources left to focus on reaching the ends of the earth. Second, we should notice that this application is based on a poor interpretation of the passage. In context, Acts 1:8 is not given to us as a model for the local church to emulate. Acts 1:8 was not intended to be a reproducible model for local churches but was given as a promise of what was going to happen with the church universal. Take note that this verse is not written in imperative form; it is not a command or a mandate. It is a bold proclamation of what is going to happen. It is a statement that the church *will* be a witness to the ends of the earth. Acts 1:8 is also a bold promise of the coming of the Holy Spirit, the source of power who will fuel the endeavor to take the witness to the whole world and all nations.

Acts 1:8 was God's idea for the first-century Christians. The rest of the book of Acts is simply the story of how God blessed these early Christians and used their efforts to reach the world — the nations and peoples — with the gospel message. As twenty-first-century followers of Christ, we now take our place as witnesses to the ends of the earth.

Don't get me wrong. I understand the tendency to look for models and easy ways of communicating a mission strategy; I'm prone to do it myself! And I know that common sense tells us that we need to focus our limited resources on local needs, to build a healthy local church first and then share the excess with the nations. But what if, by muting Christ's mandate to make disciples of all nations, we have deprived the church of the very oxygen that is required to make her healthy? What if our focus on local needs leads to unhealthy churches?

Does there have to be this conflict of interest between the local church and the nations? Not at all. In fact, they mesh perfectly. A catchphrase used lately to describe this idea — an emphasis on hybrid ministries that are simultaneously global and local — is "going glocal."

We know that our churches can be effective only where they have a presence, where people are locally rooted. No matter where we are in the world, we are called to be a conduit of the natural outflowing of Jesus through our lives to those around us. But by focusing our hearts globally, we also expand our understanding of where we are to include the ends of the earth. We embrace the full vision of the Great Commission and move one step closer to fulfilling God's purpose for his church. It's a reality of ministry that we can't minister where we don't have a presence. And to have a presence in this world, we must learn to listen to God's call and follow his heart as he leads us out of the buildings and back into the nations.

Another way to go glocal is to integrate God's passion into every aspect of ministry our churches are involved in. I'm not just talking about raising the amount of the budget we designate for the world evangelism committee or giving that missionary couple from Indonesia a little more time in the pulpit next Sunday morning. I'm talking about a change of heart that starts from the inside and works its way out, naturally, in all that we do as a church family. When entire churches get caught up in the Surge, God takes center stage and the Holy Spirit becomes the key mover and shaker in our midst. When we and our churches are properly adjusted to our biblical calling and purpose as God's people, we will experience the fullness of life that Jesus promises. Engagement in the Surge makes us consistent with our design as individuals and as the body of Christ.

Redefining Success

What is an unreached people group? An unreached people group is any population of people that is insulated from the gospel by their culture, language, geography, or politics. Unreached people groups have no native church; they lack a viable expression of Christ in their community. Because of sin and the resulting mistrust and fear that develops between people, the message about God's consuming love for all people of all nations does *not* travel naturally between different people groups. To bring the good news to unreached groups, someone has to take the initiative and step over the barrier that separates two cultures. Ralph Winter and Bruce Koch describe the challenge this way: "Even if all the members of every church in the world were to bring every one of their friends and relatives within their own culture to obedient faith in Christ, and they in turn were able to bring all of their friends and relatives to Christ and so on, no matter how much time you allow, there would still be billions cut off from the gospel. They would be sealed off by boundaries of prejudice and culture. The church cannot grow within peoples where relevant churches do not exist. Forty percent of the individuals in the world live within peoples with no church."[5]

> Shall not the low wail of helpless, hopeless misery, arising from one-half of the heathen world, pierce our sluggish ear, and rouse us, spirit, soul, and body, to one mighty, continued, unconquerable effort for China's salvation?
> — J. Hudson Taylor (1895)

Year after year, churches have been focused on counting the number of bodies that show up in their building on a Sunday morning, or the amount of money that ends up in the plate by noon. Denominational leaders may even gauge success by counting the number of buildings themselves, noting how many places of worship have opened or closed their doors. Strategies based on measuring attendance at services or counting structures are nothing more than the evangelical equivalent of the Old Testament temple strategy. Beyond the concrete reality of numbers, we have nothing but nebulous, elusive goals. Without a defined endgame — a sense of what God is doing in our midst — we often become inwardly focused and compelled by the desire to please people.

Numerical measures of success are not wrong in themselves, *if they are aligned with God's kingdom priorities.* If we are looking for some type of numerical gauge for the success of Christianity, wouldn't it make sense to measure the expansion of God's kingdom according to *his* passion and priorities? Our goals become clear as we begin to see the world as God sees it. Matthew 24:14 gives us a tangible, measurable objective that clarifies who we are and what we are to be about: "This gospel of the kingdom will be preached in the whole world as a testimony to all nations, and then the end will come."

So central is God's passion for all nations that reaching *each one* will be the indicator (or the trigger, depending on your theology) of the beginning of the end (which again means different things, depending on your personal end-time scenario). God's passion for the nations permeates Scripture from beginning to end. The challenge is to remove our traditional set of lenses through which we have viewed the purpose of the church, and put on a new set of glasses.

The great news is that God is doing a new thing in our time. What God is doing among the peoples of the world today is astounding. We can identify twenty-four thousand "nations" on earth. Our objective, as the body of Christ, is to reach each of these twenty-four thousand people groups with the life-giving message of the gospel. Take a moment to ponder just a few amazing statistics that point to this marvelous work of God developing right before our eyes:

- In 1974, nineteen thousand of these people groups were designated as "unreached peoples."
- In 1996, twelve thousand were unreached.
- Today fewer than eight thousand of these people groups are unreached.

Over the past three decades, God has been expanding his kingdom among the people groups of the world at an unprecedented rate. Not only is steady progress being made, but things are *accelerating* at a rate never before seen in history. If we do some simple math, we find:

- In 1974, five thousand people groups had viable local churches among them.

- In 1996, twelve thousand were designated as "reached."
- Today more than sixteen thousand people groups have been impacted by the Surge.

I hope this is beginning to soak in for you: *twice* as many people groups have been reached *since* 1974 (thirty-five years) as were reached in the 1,935 years *between* Pentecost and 1974.

Reached People Groups

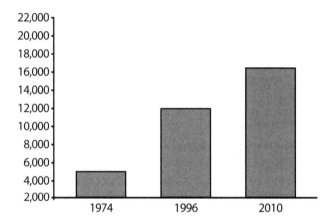

God's passion for the lost is being unleashed upon the nations in an unprecedented way today. God is closing in on the fulfillment of Matthew 28:19 – 20 and Matthew 24:14, and according to several trends we are observing, the Surge is growing in strength. As Western Christians, we may be tempted to look around and think that Christianity is on the decline. At times, serving as a leader in the Western church can feel like living in a spiritual desert. But the global church is alive and growing. As members of this worldwide body, we have a shared heritage and a common foundation. Living in the West, we also have time and we have resources. And most important, we have a God who is committed to finishing the work he began long ago!

Learning to see the world as God sees it and then understanding ourselves afresh in light of what he is doing — it's nothing short of a defining moment for our ministries. Matthew 28:19–20 (the Great Commission) can be found in nearly every evangelical church constitution. It's plastered on our walls and in our bulletins and brochures. But what are we really doing to join God in this awesome work?

> The body of believers carries a sense of holy trust from God, that God has given them a holy task that they are to pursue to completion.... Now more than ever, he is summoning forth the awesome beauty and capacity that he has deposited among his people worldwide.
>
> — George Miley

This is the great paradigm shift that underlies this entire book, and that's why I'm going to ask you to really stop and think about this for a moment. God's passion for the nations of our world — the unreached people without a gospel witness — is not a secondary concern. It is the pervasive theme of God's purposeful love flowing throughout history and throughout the Scriptures. This movement of God's love — what we have been calling the Surge — is flowing along his ordained timeline for humanity, pulsing incessantly in the veins of those whose hearts beat by the power of his Holy Spirit. As our churches awaken to this reality, we become strategic players, rather than incidental pawns, in the consuming drama of the ages.

I am convinced that Christ is the hope of a dying, desperate, and deluded world. Because the church carries with her the life, love, and message of Christ, the church delivers that hope. But it's more than a one-way transaction. As the church delivers this message of hope, we begin to discover and experience our true purpose, the fulfillment of God's joyful plan for his people. Could it be not only that the unreached people groups of our world need the hope of Christ that we carry with us but also that we really need them as well, to be all that God intends us to be?

Chapter Three

First Things First

The Why and the How of the Surge

> Unless there is a still center in the middle of the storm,
> unless a person in the midst of all their activities pre-
> serves a secret room in their heart where they stand alone
> before God, unless we do this we will lose all sense of
> spiritual direction and be torn to pieces.
>
> — *Anonymous fourth-century desert monk*

The story is told of a distinguished explorer who spent a number of years with the natives of the Amazon. On one excursion, the explorer and the natives made extraordinary speed for the first two days, but on the third morning when it was time to start, all the natives sat down looking very solemn and made no preparations to leave. "They are waiting," the chief explained to the explorer. "They cannot move farther until their souls have caught up with their bodies." That's a great story that raises the question, Were these men acting on a truth we have forgotten? Are we in chaos because we have forgotten to wait for our souls?

In the pages ahead, I'm going to lay out before you a series of innovations that are propelling the Surge forward with astonishing power and speed. The resources and opportunities that are available may revolutionize your ministry — or perhaps overwhelm you. We'll talk about networks of leadership, sharing of ideas and tools for communicating vision, and developing personalized strategies for mobilizing our local congregations for the global cause. In the next chapter, we will even explore one aspect of applied technology that with just a few mouse clicks can launch you and your congregation — at no cost — right into the very heart of the Surge.

With all of the contemporary possibilities comes an ancient and deceitful temptation: in any great spiritual endeavor lies the danger of getting so caught up in the work that we forget our first love, leaving behind the life-giving waters of the gospel. Before jumping headfirst into these next chapters, let's take some time to look at our hearts, examine our motives, and talk about the why that comes before the how.

Finding Our Place

We are recipients and partakers of the Surge, first and foremost. This divine order makes all the difference. We ignore it at great peril. We align our lives to it with incredible blessing. The nature of authentic worship and ministry is to first (and always) come and rest before God — listening, trusting, and, particularly, enjoying him. We must first (and continually) submerse ourselves in his mercy and grace in broken dependence. Then, when it comes time to act, our proclamation to the nations will naturally flow out of our lives as we walk in the way he has prepared: "On the last and greatest day of the Feast, Jesus stood and said in a loud voice, 'If anyone is thirsty, let him come to me and drink. Whoever believes in me, as the Scripture has said, streams of living water will flow from within him'" (John 7:37 – 38).

What a tragedy it would be if our enthusiasm for God's redeeming work in this world did nothing but fuel more legalistic activity, adding to the things that keep us so busy and leave us feeling so empty. We must never forget that the Surge is for our benefit. God can make the stones cry out if he wants to reach the world with the truth. *We need him, not the other way around.* We are not saved for a cause or a program; we are invited into God's global plans because they are part of our cure — God's means of redeeming us, transforming us, and revealing the Spirit of Christ alive in us.

Often, when the story of Mary and Martha welcoming Jesus into their home (Luke 10) is preached, the application is that we need to find a balance between frantically working for God and quietly resting at his feet. But I think that misses the heart of what Jesus says to Martha when she confronts him with her frustration and irritation at her sister. Jesus says, "Martha … you are worried and upset about many things, but *only one thing* is needed" (Luke 10:41 – 42, emphasis added). Jesus reminds Martha — and us today — that the cure for a frantic heart is found in recognizing the simplicity of the Christian life. Jesus asks Martha to remember only one thing, the thing she needs most: to rest in him. This is not a call to passivity or laziness; it is a reminder of the priority of relationship. If Jesus had asked Mary to get him some food, she would have joyfully jumped at the opportunity to serve. Instead Jesus encourages her to prioritize intimacy *with* him over doing things *for* him. The secret of our salvation is dependence — learning to rest in Christ, living in the power and strength he provides by his Spirit. It's about living for his glory and not wasting time seeking our own. Let me warn you up front — living this way is not simply difficult; it's impossible!

Only one person has ever lived this way consistently, without fail, and the good news is that he now lives in you (Gal. 2:20). The secret to longevity in ministry, to finding consistent joy and passion for this mission we call the Surge, is to live each day surrendered to Christ. The call to enter the Surge is a call to surrender fully to Christ, who indwells you. Unless we experience his life in us, we will grow tired, frustrated, bitter, and angry when our resources are exhausted and our plans for building our own church have failed.

All this might sound like I'm dismissing everything I've just said to you about our need to get involved in God's work, to join him in his passion for a lost world, to answer the call he gives us to reach every nation with the life-giving presence of a vibrant church and the truth of the gospel. Let me clarify what I'm getting at: we need to have the right why before we jump into the how of ministry. Doing the right thing for the wrong reasons will inevitably lead to failure, burnout, and discouragement. There are two key questions you should ask yourself as you examine your heart and your ministry:

1. Am I doing all this *for* God? (In other words, are you motivated to serve out of a sense of obligation, a sense of duty, or in an effort to earn God's favor and love?)
2. Or is he doing this *through* me? (Is the work you do evidence of something God has done in your life, something that he continues to work in you and through you as you surrender your life to him each day?)

If you're doing this *for* God, your efforts in the Surge will become just one more formula, one more program, one more burden to add to your "to do" list. Sadly, your efforts may even (unintentionally) become a new standard for your own self-righteousness — something that you use to judge the spirituality and commitment of other people as you compare yourself with them. Most significant, reaching the nations *for* God will rob you of the blessings provided by the very message that you devotedly proclaim to the world. Ultimately, if reaching the world becomes a performance to please God, it will fail. Leaders, pastors, and missionaries in today's church need to take seriously the message that Christ gave to the first-century church in Ephesus: "I know your deeds, your hard work and your perseverance.... *[You have performed diligently in order to share the truth about me with every* ethne *on the planet.]* You have persevered and have endured hardships for my name, and have not grown weary. Yet I hold this against you: You have forsaken your first love. Remember the height from which you have fallen! Repent and do the things you did at first. If you do not repent, I will come to you and remove your lampstand from its place" (Rev. 2:2 – 5).

Notice that the second question frames our work and ministry in a different way: Is God doing this through me? If so, it changes everything! We recognize the priority of our relationship with him, and we remember the mercy and grace that saved us from our fallen state. We are continually

> If your greatest joy is to experience the indwelling grace of God overflowing from you for the good of others, then the best news in all the world is that God will do the impossible through you for the salvation of the hidden peoples. "With men it is impossible, but not with God; for all things are possible with God."
>
> — John Piper, *Desiring God*

enamored by the fact that we have been crucified with Christ, that he lives in us, that he is the one who produces fruit through us. Our job is to open ourselves up to be conduits of that same force that gave us life in the first place: Jesus. Our devotion to being witnesses to the ends of the earth is not an act of self-generated determination and strength. If we understand and accept that Christ desires to live his life through us, we will discover that we can do all things through him — even fulfill the Great Commission.

But if we don't ...

Empty Together

I walked back to my office and closed the door, the words of my elders echoing in my mind. I felt alone. No, that's not honest enough: I felt completely abandoned, crushed, and defeated, and I was convinced there was no one who could relate to me. My elders, who were also my friends, had just leveled me with a disappointing evaluation. This was coupled with staff conflicts and personal exhaustion.

I knew I was done. Picking up the phone, I called my chairman. "Kurt, I am going away for three days. I am not preaching this Sunday. Pray for me." After making arrangements for someone to fill the pulpit, I walked out the door — and wondered if I would ever return. I went to a nature preserve near the church and sat alone by a stream, the water slowly flowing by as I prayed, cried, read, and listened. I returned to the creek the next day. And the next. Alone.

> When I left England, my hope of India's conversion was very strong; but amongst so many obstacles, it would die, unless upheld by God. Well, I have God, and his Word is true.
>
> — William Carey (1793)

Burnout is the product of every human machine, and sadly, that includes institutional Christianity. Churches continually ride that fine line between being a life-giving organism of grace and being a life-sucking institution. I had allowed Bent Tree to become a place that was draining me of life, and in the midst of my time alone, I sensed that Jesus was beckoning me back: "Come to me, all you who are weary and burdened, and I will give you rest. Take my yoke upon you and learn from me, for I am gentle and humble in heart, and you will find rest for your souls. For my yoke is easy and my burden is light" (Matt. 11:28 – 30).

I realize you've probably heard this passage and have possibly even taught on it several times. But let me ask you an honest question: do you partake of the rest you proclaim to others? The Surge — this grand movement of God's mercy, grace, and compassion for the world — is being poured out all around this planet. If you are to join what God is doing *out* there, it must be *in* you. It's not enough to know that it's happening or that it's available. To be a minister of God's life-giving water to others, you must yourself be immersed in it. Are you personally submerged, swimming in the wonders of the mercy and grace of God? Are you a *partaker* or just a *proclaimer*?

Drain Cycle

In his book *Grace Walk*, Steve McVey describes what he calls the "motivation-condemnation-rededication cycle." It goes like this: I hear a great sermon, or read a story about a saint from the 1800s who spent his time from 2:00 a.m. to 5:00 a.m. praying, and I get all motivated. Then I set a preposterous goal (like reaching the unreached people groups of the world), assuming that if I meet it, God will be pleased with me. *Part of his pleasure will certainly overflow into our ministry here at home*, I think. *God's blessing will flow, perhaps leading to increased attendance and a cool new building.* At the end of the day, the success of my ministry rests on whether I can crawl out of bed in the middle of the night to pray. So I am *motivated*!

Then I fail. Of course I fail, because I am trying to do life in my own strength, and Paul is clear in his letters that I am bound to fail if I attempt to live out personal faith in my own strength (he calls it "living according to the flesh"). But because I think God's pleasure in me and my ministry success are tied to my performance, my failure is

> When we look at ourselves, at the littleness of our love, the bareness of our service and the small progress we make toward perfection, how soul refreshing it is to turn away to Him.
>
> — J. Hudson Taylor (1854)

triply hard to take. My self-condemnation and the increasing volume of condemning voices around me (do you have any in your church?) overwhelm me. So I *rededicate* myself and try harder the next time. All this guarantees that my future failure will be even more painful. Sound familiar? It is a devastating trap for pastors and church leaders, and many of us have become ensnared by this pattern of relating to God.

The mistake each of us makes is believing that we *earn* God's pleasure and blessing by performing well, when the truth is that we already *have* God's favor. It is a free gift of his grace, given to us through the sacrifice of Jesus Christ, and is not based on any aspect of our performance. The truth that you must continually be reminded of is that God approves of you and is pleased with you, not based on what you do but because of what Jesus has already done. I know you preach that to others, but do you partake of it yourself?

Really?

Whether your church has five thousand people or fifty, whether your attendance is increasing or decreasing, whether you are praying or sleeping in — even whether you are involved in reaching the unreached people of this world — God is not scoring you on your performance. God's concerns are less complicated than ours. In Galatians 5:6, Paul reminds us that "the only thing that counts is faith expressing itself through love." This is what God cares about: faith. *Are you trusting me today?* he asks. *Are you trusting me to live and love powerfully through you today?*

> God is most glorified in us when we are most satisfied in him. This is perhaps the most important sentence in my theology.
> — John Piper, *Let the Nations Be Glad!*

Reclaiming Identity

God will call us to do many different things, to different-sized churches and differently shaped ministries. He will call some of us to rich places and others to poor ones. *There are so many variables, it is preposterous to attempt to place a grid of human success over all ministries.*

This cuts to the core question of our identity:

- Who am I? Who am I *really*? Please don't define me by how I look or what I say or where you find me standing on any given Sunday morning or Wednesday night.

- Who are you? I realize that this might seem like a very simple and fundamental question, but the answer forms the rock-solid foundation upon which everything in life is built. We *never* graduate from the powerful identity truths that define who we really are.

"I have been crucified with Christ and I no longer live, but Christ lives in me. The life I live in the body, I live by faith in the Son of God, who loved me and gave himself for me" (Gal. 2:20). This is the great mystery, isn't it! Nearly two thousand years ago, on a hill outside of Jerusalem, a great exchange took place. God transcended time and space when we died on Calvary with Christ so that he can live in us today with all his power, peace, and wisdom. The implications are phenomenal. There is therefore no condemnation for those who are in Christ (Rom. 8:1 – 2). Our failures and shortcomings, as filthy as they might be, have been washed white as the snow (Isa. 1:18). We can run as adopted children into the arms of our "Abba" (Rom. 8:15; Gal. 4:6), set free time and time again as we were during that first season of faith when his grace and mercy was fresh and new.

> You are already clean because of the word I have spoken to you. Remain in me, and I will remain in you. No branch can bear fruit by itself; it must remain in the vine. Neither can you bear fruit unless you remain in me. I am the vine; you are the branches. If a man remains in me and I in him, he will bear much fruit; apart from me you can do nothing.
>
> — *John 15:3 – 5*

Those are red-letter words — Jesus' timeless message to us today. Christ is the core of the grapevine, and we are simply its branches. If we are to bear any genuine fruit in our lives, it is because he has produced it through us; without him we can't do anything.

> We are His workmanship, created in Christ Jesus for good works, which God prepared beforehand so that we would walk in them.
>
> — *Ephesians 2:10 (NASB)*

You may wonder why I've included this chapter in a book for leaders, a book focused on fulfilling the Great Commission and understanding the gloriously global love of God for the nations.

> **Christ in us is the seed of the next generation. The difference this seed can leave in the soil of a people group is significant.**
> — Neil Cole

I've included it for those of you who (like me) look at God's commission to us, his call to reach the nations with the message of the gospel and disciple them, and feel intimidated, reluctant, and uncertain about what *you* should be doing! Let me encourage you: God has this entire thing planned out. He is in charge, working all things according to his purposes. The Surge is not something we have to invent or program or plan — it's a wild ride on the wave of God's love for the world. Reaching the nations is *God's* work, and we are simply the means he will use to accomplish what he wants to do.

Much of this became clear to me while I was inner tubing down a river with my family in Wisconsin. If you just sit back and relax in the tube, it can be a nice experience. You gently paddle as the current takes you where it wants to flow. But as soon as I would get off the inner tube and try standing on my feet in the river, I would feel the force of the water pushing against me. If you aren't careful and the current is strong, you can get knocked over and your feet can get lodged under rocks. People will sometimes drown when they try to stand up against the flow of the current. But feet up, floating in the surge of the current, it feels like you are secure and the entire world is revolving slowly beneath you. It's a relatively effortless ride when you give in to the force of the river.

The "work" of serving God is this: we simply trust in him, listen to him, and obey his Word to us. We ride the wave of his love for the world.

May the God of peace, who through the blood of the eternal covenant brought back from the dead our Lord Jesus, that great Shepherd of the sheep, equip you with everything good for doing his will, and may he work in us what is pleasing to him, through Jesus Christ, to whom be glory for ever and ever. Amen.

— *Hebrews 13:20 – 21*

We should find ourselves constantly pushing back from the planning table (full of diagrams and statistics) at our meetings and take time to revel in speechless awe at the amazing God who has saved us. There must be a break in our professionalism, a shattering of the illusion that we have somehow mastered this message. Our effectiveness in the Surge really begins when we are launched back into wonder that Jesus loves *us.*

> A vision of the possibilities — including past victories, present world trends, available personnel, money, and resources — should never overshadow the clear biblical principle that when we are weak then we really are strong because God's power is allowed full expression through our weakness (2 Corinthians 12:9 – 10).
>
> — David Bryant, *In the Gap*

Meanwhile, Back at the Creek

I'm not sure that I would have come to see how far I had wandered from these core, foundational truths if it had not been for my elders' devastating evaluation and the struggles at our church. Alone at the nature preserve, I wandered through the trees. I felt like I had given God sixteen good years and now I had reached the end. Sitting by a small stream, I told the Lord, "I don't know what else I can do for you. I have tried so hard. I have worked so hard and for so long, and now everything seems to be falling apart. What am I missing?"

At that moment, I sensed the Spirit whispering to me: *Pete, am I enough for you? Pete, if you were never to preach another sermon, never to lead Bent Tree again, never to "do ministry" again, never to be recognized ... would Jesus be enough for you?*

That's the question that makes all the difference. Innovative ideas, new strategies for missions, new paradigms for outreach — none of them make a difference if you can't answer this one question: *Is Jesus enough for me?*

Theologically, you know the correct answer to that question. But before you jump into the Surge and immerse yourself in innovative strategies for reaching the world, take the time to ask it once more: *Is Jesus enough for me?*

It took a ministry crisis for me to realize that I really didn't believe that Jesus was enough. David *walked* with God, but his son Solomon *worked* for God. Which of these two was described as a man after God's own heart? I realized that I had been working for God, trying to create my own identity apart from the life of Christ he has graciously given me. I had become so consumed trying to manage the Surge that I forgot to partake of it myself. That day, alone in the woods, I realized that my primary identity in life does not lie in pastoring a growing church, innovating new ministries, or working tirelessly for the kingdom. My primary call and responsibility is to cultivate an intimate walk with the Jesus, who lives in me, and then allowing him to live, love, and lead through me.

In the moments afterward, sitting by the stream, I felt again the refreshing rains of God's love upon my heart. The heavy yoke of my self-effort was lifted from my weary shoulders, and the perfect-fitting, gentle yoke of Christ took its place; and I found, one more time, the promised rest for my soul.

Then, in a quiet voice, the Spirit spoke again: *Now go back, trust me, and lead as if you have nothing to lose.*

Part Two

WAVES

Look at the nations and watch —
and be utterly amazed. For I am going
to do something in your days that you
would not believe, even if you were told.
— Habakkuk 1:5

Chapter Four

Virtual Flood

Surging through the Digital Age

We are the first generation in all of human history to hold in our hands the technology to reach every man, woman, and child on earth.... This is not a distant dream. It is a current reality. Market forces in technology are driving us forward.

— *Walt Wilson, Global Media Outreach*

Sarah grew up in a churchgoing family, but she spent most of her life sitting back, listening to messages on Sundays, and watching others do the work of mission. All of that changed three years ago when she answered God's call upon her life and became immersed in the global movement of the Savior's love.

Sarah has been caught up in the Surge.

Since then, Sarah has shared God's love with over fourteen hundred people from a wide variety of unreached people groups on every continent. It's difficult to measure the impact her life is having for God's kingdom. In addition to her personal ministry, Sarah is leading a team of fifteen individuals who are working to make a difference in the lives of those in need on a daily basis — in virtually every corner of the globe. Her life and ministry affect thousands of other lives each and every day.

Amazingly, Sarah does all of this without ever leaving the country. She doesn't even leave her home state, and she rarely strays from the town she grew up in. In fact, most of the time, she never even leaves her house. And that's the way it has to be. Because, you see, Sarah can't walk; she can't dress herself; she can't feed herself. Sarah can't even talk.

Meet the newest breed of missionaries. Welcome to missions in the digital age.

A Word Redefined

You may have noticed that I have intentionally avoided using the term *missionary* in this book as much as possible. There are several reasons for this. First of all, the word *missions* doesn't appear anywhere in the Scriptures. The words we translate as "evangelist" (Eph. 4:11) and "witness" (Acts 1:8) come closest in meaning to what we commonly refer to as "missionary." Even though the words *missions* and *missionary* are not used in the Bible, it is clear that both the priority and the process of reaching the nations for Christ are revealed everywhere throughout the Scriptures (for example, see Prov. 14:25 – 27; Isa. 6:8; Acts 10:43; 14:17). We see all sorts of cross-cultural and international spreading of the Word of God in the Old Testament (see passages such as Josh. 2:18 – 19; 2 Kings 5:2 – 4; Jonah 1:2; 3:2). Even the Psalms contain passages that emphasize the theme of proclaiming God's glory among the nations of the world. Psalm 96 is sometimes referred to as a missionary song, though, again, the word *missionary* never appears in this psalm.

Today God is still calling his people to be ambassadors of Christ (Rom. 1:14 – 16; 2 Cor. 5:20), assuring us of the presence of Christ always (Matt. 28:20; Heb. 13:5). We are entrusted with the gospel (1 Thess. 2:4), sent forth (John 17:18) through open doors (1 Cor. 16:9), and propelled into "the regions beyond" (2 Cor. 10:16), where we are to preach the gospel (Acts 10:42 – 43) as it is defined in 1 Corinthians 15:1 – 4. We work under divine compulsion and use every means possible (1 Cor. 9:16, 22.), including prayer (2 Cor. 1:11) and support from the home churches (1 Cor. 16:1 – 2), as we endeavor with God (2 Cor. 6:1) to fulfill his eternal purpose, which is to be known and worshiped by disciples of all nations (Matt. 28:19).

God's Word has plenty to say about the goal and process of how his message of grace and mercy is to be spread to all nations, but it never uses the words *mission* or *missionary* at all. These are simply words we have created to summarize this distinctive, biblical teaching.

As with many words today, the meaning of the word *missions* is changing. Most likely, you've heard rumblings about the "missional church" movement. In his book *Confessions of a Reformission Rev.: Hard Lessons from an Emerging Missional Church*, Mark Driscoll redefines the use of the word *missions*: "The end of Christendom and the transition to a post-Christian culture is currently dominated by the *contemporary and evangelical church*, which is marked by the following common trait: Missions is a church department that sends people and money to foreign countries.... With Christendom essentially winding down now in the United States and officially over in Europe ... the *emerging and missional church* is marked by the following traits: Missions is every Christian being a missionary to their local culture."[6]

You'll notice that Driscoll is reemphasizing an oft-neglected truth — that every believer is called to respond to God's purpose for the church by reaching out to those who are lost and without the gospel. This certainly includes those in our own neighborhoods and cities. I endorse what Mark is saying about this in his book — his message is thought-provoking, innovative, powerful, and mobilizing, and it needs to be heard. But as important as it is to emphasize evangelism to those in our local culture, that's not the definition of *missions* I want to promote in this book. Nor am I talking about *missions* and *missionaries* in the traditional sense of the words — a narrowly conceived understanding of iconic men and women of faith who donned pith helmets and headed for the jungle.

Missions can be a confusing and easily misunderstood term, but it's hard to avoid using it in a discussion like this. At the very least, avoiding the term would force me to leave out some really powerful quotes about God's love for the nations. For example, in the opening paragraphs of his classic book on the theology of missions, *Let the Nations Be Glad!* John Piper writes, "Missions exists because worship doesn't." I have a hard time coming up with my own quote that sounds half as good, so I'm going to continue using the term *mission* simply because other men and women have used it to express biblical truth so eloquently! Just remember that when I use words like *mission* and *missionary*, I'm referring to the broader perspective of redemptive history — what we call the Surge — this global movement of our Savior's love, redeeming individuals and entire nations for the fulfillment of God's eternal purpose.

These are new days for the church. We live in a new world of opportunities. God is doing a new thing in our midst. Preconceived and outdated notions of missions and missionaries *must* be left behind, or we will be limited by what we are comfortable doing, the familiar patterns of the past. Conventional wisdom, in many cases, *needs* to be abandoned. In the chapters ahead, we are going to look at a series of innovative transformations, made possible through the networking leaders, that can pull you and your congregation off the dusty shores of Western Christianity and into the Surge. It's time to begin thinking outside the box of traditional missions.

Going Virtual

Sarah is a beautiful example of how these innovative transformations in our understanding of missions are being practically lived out in the lives of individuals. Sarah is a remarkable person whose body has been twisted by cerebral palsy. Every day, she and her mother face countless challenges that most of us will never know about or experience. So how is God using her to reach thousands of people all over the world? Early each morning, Sarah wakes up and her mother, Pat, comes in to feed her, bathe her, and dress her. Later, after being wheeled to her computer, Sarah uses a specially designed peg to type one letter at a time. Letter by letter, word by word, one email at a time, God works through her to impact the nations. While it can cost thousands of dollars to train and send missionaries out to live in foreign lands, Sarah is one of the most cost-effective, resource-efficient world-changers on the planet. This beautiful young woman in a wheelchair is a wonderful model of effective, efficient outreach.

Sarah's ministry represents a megashift in the nature of the Surge. The timeless mandate of ancient Scriptures to take the good news to all nations is taking on new realities in the information age, in which the spread of the gospel can be measured in terabytes and bandwidth — and the impact on the church is astounding. Sarah teaches each of us that there are no limitations to our ability to respond to God's call. It is possible to be a part of the exponentially expanding outflow of God's passion for the world without ever leaving your office or living room.

> The upbuilding of the church ought to be variously accommodated to the customs of each nation and age, it will be fitting on (as the advantage of the church will require) to change and abrogate traditional practices and to establish new ones. Indeed, I admit that we ought not to charge into innovation rashly, suddenly, for insufficient cause. But level best to judge what may hurt or edify; and if we let love be our guide, all will be safe.
>
> — John Calvin (1556)

Walt Wilson, the founder of Global Media Outreach, calls this "the shift from atoms to bits": "The place to begin is an understanding that the internet — the world of 'bits' — is a real place, just like any physical place constructed of atoms. It cannot be ignored since it is inhabited by over one billion human beings in every country on earth. It has grown by about one million people every day.... They live in the world of cyberspace so much so that they no longer view the internet, the smart phone, or their laptop as a technology. They view it as an ordinary, everyday tool."[7]

We have been hearing this type of sensationalist language for the past fifteen years, but when we strip away the hype of the internet, the question still remains: do we get it? Do the leaders of the church in this age *really* get it? When the internet first became popular in the early nineties, a handful of Christian ministries immediately took notice. They created Christian websites, sites that functioned as electronic brochures for churches and ministries. (We were all pretty proud that we had exchanged smoke signals for a website and an email address.) It was certainly a good start, but unfortunately most of us went back to our ministry as usual even as the applied technology continued to blast ahead at light speed. This shift from atoms to bits — the physical to the digital — is sometimes referred to as a *radical discontinuity*, a change that happens so fast that the human mind doesn't know how to describe it (let alone forecast it or harness it).

Still, we did the best we could at the time. In 1997, the Billy Graham Center (Wheaton, Illinois) hosted a consultation on internet evangelism that led to the formation of the Internet Evangelism Coalition (IEC) in 1999 and the creation of Internet Evangelism Day *(www.internetevangelismday.com)*. IEC partners have also developed the Evangelism Toolbox *(www.evangelismtoolbox. com)*, a massive and ever-expanding database of resources that can be used to help people share their faith. It's a phenomenal conglomeration of multilingual, multiformat evangelism resources provided by many of the top evangelical organizations around the world, in both online and offline formats. Several courses are offered, including online training for internet evangelists.

Eventually websites became more interactive and began reaching out rather than just providing information and resources. Sites like Jesus2020.com, LifesGreatestQuestion.com, and GodLoves-TheWorld.com are great examples of websites that form a bridge, taking the visitor from topics of interest and leading them to the gospel.[8]

Recently I partnered with a network of pastors and ministries from the Dallas area to help create iamsecond.com. We gathered video testimonies from Dallas locals who have made Jesus Christ *first* in their lives, and in them they explain why "I am second" to him. Stories on the site include the testimonies of Brian Welch from the rock band Korn, NASCAR superstar Darrel Waltrip, politician Mike Huckabee, and others (including yours truly). On the "privacy" of the internet, I spill my guts and share one of my deep personal struggles for the whole world to see! Visitors to this site can also find practical answers to some of life's most difficult questions. Those who want follow-up can either connect with someone online or have their contact information forwarded to

> Each medium provides another layer of global coverage. Not every layer will affect every person equally, but the cumulative multiplicity of media layers does give us grounds to give greater expectation that the task can be finished if we mobilize the resources of the church.
>
> — Patrick Johnstone

an I Am Second group in their local area.

Not surprisingly, this stuff is working! Not long ago I finished preaching at our second service and was greeted by a rather disheveled man who smelled like a twelve-hour-old martini. "Hi, I'm here ...," he said. I replied, "Nice to meet you. What brought you to Bent Tree?" He told me his name and continued, "I was driving down the street, saw the I Am Second billboard, went to the website, saw your testimony, and decided to come for a visit. What do I do now?" After a few minutes of conversation, our new friend was enveloped by loving church members while I made my way back to a pizza luncheon for our first-time visitors. As I sat at one of the tables, I asked each person at the lunch to share the story of how they arrived at Bent Tree. A young guy with a killer smile, some cool tats, and facial piercings said, "I was driving down the road, and I saw a billboard that said, "I am second," so I went to the website, saw your story, and decided to come. I don't know what I think of all this Jesus stuff, but *trying to be first* is getting old ..." Just this past week I spoke at an I Am Second Bible study at my son's public high school. Every Friday morning, a group of kids gather before school, watch one of the videos on the site, and then discuss it together. This program is run completely by students — students who saw the videos, liked them, and wanted to share them with their friends.

The website iamsecond.com illustrates one of the paradoxes of the internet: it's a place where people can search and share with "worldwide anonymity." Seekers from various nations are now searching for God on the internet rather than looking for him in a traditional church. The internet is now one of the primary connection points for those coming *into* the church. Large numbers of people are also discovering "virtual churches" — an entirely different way of developing relationships, experiencing fellowship, and engaging in discipleship than would have been conceivable just twenty years ago.

As this shift from atoms to bits continues, it is leading to global transformations that may render much of our conventional thinking about missions obsolete. Even as I write about these changes, I am exposing the limitations of the old world. Paper-and-ink books are being replaced by electronic and digital media that can be distributed rapidly and exponentially. The radical discontinuity we are experiencing in the world of outreach and global missions means that some of the examples I give in this chapter will quickly become dated. Only one thing is certain: what is cutting-edge today will be commonplace tomorrow — and likely obsolete the day after that. Today email is giving way to texting; MySpace is being overshadowed by FaceBook; Christians are using Twitter during worship services, and eBay (the biggest flea market in the world) looks like it may soon give way to Craig and his list. Tomorrow these transforming technologies will undoubtedly be superseded by the next generation of latest and greatest innovations.

So be it! Our world is incalculably different than the world of two thousand or even two hundred years ago. To a very large extent, geographical distinctions and limitations have been changed by advances in transportation, communication, and access to instant information. Statistics change so frequently that I'm going to avoid specific numbers, but suffice it to say that we are looking at *bil-*

lions of internet users. According to Google executives, *millions* of people conduct a search on spiritual terms every day. Pew Internet and the American Life Project recently reported that nearly two-thirds of online Americans use the internet in search of spiritual meaning and religious activities. Our neighbors are seeking answers, but in most cases the church will be the *last* place they will go for those answers. And around the world, there are still multitudes who don't even have a church they can go to, and some would likely be arrested or killed for openly seeking Christ.

Many of these seekers are people in the midst of crisis. Pollster George Barna reports that about one-third of people in a given community are facing difficult, life-altering situations. They are flocking to the web (instead of the church), looking for a place to share their problems with others and find solutions. They are seeking safety in the anonymous intimacy provided by the internet. They come to a site seeking relief from their pain, looking for comfort, not knowing that there is a Comforter who loves them.

And many are finding him through a website or an online testimony.

The strategy that many Christians and Christian organizations are adopting is deceptively simple: individuals, churches, and parachurch ministries are creating websites and other forms of social media that give people the opportunity to find real answers to their questions.

GMO and U

Global Media Outreach (GMO) has created nearly one hundred websites that use internet-based outreach and communication technologies in text, video, and audio on multiple platforms. Through the use of computers, iPods, iPads, cell phones, podcasting, internet radio, and other emerging communication technologies, plus TV and film, they are reaching out to the nations. And the nations are reaching back. There's no way to track the progress they are making with individual people groups at this time, but they report seekers visiting their sites from every one of the approximately 220 political nations on the globe. Here are just a few of the millions of responses they see each year on their sites:

> Please pray for my emotional healing. My 5-year-old daughter died a few weeks ago in a car accident. I was raising her alone. I have attempted to take my life two times these past weeks. I am in a care facility. I am not a Christian, but know God will hear your prayers on my behalf.
>
> *— Young woman in England*

> I'm thirty-two and I've never been so lost in my life. I just want to give up and die; the only thing that keeps me going is my 7-year-old son. I need help. I do not know how to start or what to do.
>
> *— Woman in Nice, France*

> I am Muslim but I want to be Christian, so which kind of help will you do? I'm thinking about myself after the changing of my religion. I have become tired from this area's situation and all the day they pass their time; like in suicide attack.
>
> *— Man in Pakistan*

> I belong to Hindu family. We were been into idol worship. I am the only one in my family accept Jesus as my personal saviour and my lord.
>
> *— "S," Andhra Pradesh, India*

> I need the love and mercy of God ... And I need Jesus as my saviour.
>
> *— "B," Saudi Arabia*

> I am just so happy to be accidentally open this site ... maybe God had showed me the way to him.
>
> *— "P," Philippines*

About one out of every five seekers who visit a site indicates a decision for Christ after working through a gospel presentation. In fact, you can watch this happen! The activity occurring on the GMO family of websites has been superimposed onto the globe of Google Earth in real time and is accessible (as of this printing) at *www.GMOEarth.com*. It's stunning to observe as seekers and decision makers find Christ at every end of the earth. We are truly witnessing the fulfillment of Acts 1:8 right before our eyes!

Seekers who want to find out more are enrolled in a thirty-day devotional study. Those who indicate a decision for Christ are introduced to another website that answers questions and helps them grow as followers of Christ: iChristianLife.com.

Presenting the gospel to someone is an important first step, but connecting a new believer to a local church is the key to helping that person grow as a Christian. Matthew 28 is a call for us to make disciples, not just converts. Even those who come to know Christ out of an unreached people group are now members of the greater body of Christ and will need to find their place in the universal church.

About one out of every six people who indicate making a decision for Christ on the GMO family of websites seeks personal follow-up through email, so GMO has developed a unique response system that can securely empower thousands of people to serve as online missionaries, personally sharing their faith one-on-one through the internet as they respond to seekers and decision makers. This presents one of the most innovative, powerful, and urgent opportunities for the local church to enter into the work that God is doing among the nations!

The response to sites like these has been accelerating so quickly that today's numbers will be out of date tomorrow. And quite frankly, they are too big for us to wrap our heads around anyway. Tens of millions of people are visiting the GMO websites alone, and millions are indicating decisions for Christ, with hundreds of thousands of those decisions resulting in an ongoing email relationship. Through a relationship with an online missionary, these new believers begin the discipleship journey and eventually connect to a church or a Christian movement within his or her country. The experience is obviously transformational for these new believers, but it's also changing the lives of those who serve as online missionaries. More and more people are realizing that they can be used by God (right where they live) as he works through them to reach the nations — through the internet. One online missionary described one of his experiences:

> I shared with a Catholic seminarian studying to be a priest in Kenya. He asked, "Can you help me understand how to have a personal relationship with Jesus? I've asked my professors and they cannot tell me." I shared with him over the course of two weeks having him use the online resources of the 4 Laws and the Holy Spirit Booklet. He wrote back and said, "Thank you so much for helping me understand how to have a relationship with Jesus and how to live a life empowered by the Holy Spirit. About four months ago a middle-aged woman from the Netherlands came into my box searching more for God. She was a Christian but had been out of touch of a church and such — basically was kind of dry. I talked to her some and encouraged her to go to church, not really thinking she would do anything. But through a period of four months she has started consistently going to church, even serves with other ladies cleaning up the church during the week, and is growing in the Lord. We still correspond, and I find her heart so sweet. It is encouraging to know that we really do have an impact on people's lives!"

What's happening in the world of bits and bytes is somewhat akin to the practice of door-to-door evangelism (everybody's favorite evangelism strategy), but with an important difference: *a world of hungry seekers is coming to your house, through the internet, begging to be told about Jesus.* These are people who aren't darkening the door of the church, but Jesus is still knocking on their door ... and now the internet has brought them to *our* door.

As internet evangelism explodes all around us, the need for personal online missionaries has never been greater. Tragically, thousands of emails from seekers go unanswered every day because there simply aren't enough people to follow up with them. Church leaders are beginning to realize that this is a rare opportunity to be involved in the unprecedented work God is doing to reach the world. Many leaders wisely recognize that things are changing so quickly that it's possible this opportunity will not last forever. Many cults are also seizing this technology for their own purposes, and they are frequently well funded and well staffed.

Yet for those who are willing to dream big, the possibilities seem almost endless.

Joel Hunter, senior pastor of multisite Northland Community Church *(www.northlandchurch.net)*, calls this the most exciting ministry opportunity he has seen in forty years. To start things off at their church, Northland did three orientations to the online missionary program: one for their staff and two for their congregation. Currently Northland has 250 online missionaries doing internet evangelism through Global Media Outreach. In 2009, these virtual missionaries responded to more than ninety-one thousand seekers from around the world. But that's just the beginning of their vision. Dr. Dan Lacich, an associate at Northland, explains: "We were a multisite asking, 'Where now?' We were experimenting with new ideas. Our senior pastor felt impressed that we were to be a catalyst for a multitude of new churches around the globe. We call them 'simple churches' that could be drawn together anywhere, and we had thought that ten thousand was a reasonable vision."

As part of that vision, Northland is launching SimplyChurch.com, an online training site for those who come to faith around the world and have no church in their community. Northland's goal is to have the website content translated into multiple languages so that new believers from unreached people groups can start home churches in their own communities. "Anything we do for equipping or training must be deliverable through a cell phone. That's how the world will now access the internet," Dan explains. "We've never felt like our materials belong to us, and we want them to be available for free to any individual or church anywhere on the planet."

Their aspirations seemed to fit a God-sized vision for the church, until the day Northland hosted a church planting conference. While eavesdropping on one of the sessions, Joel Hunter was challenged to pray about how many churches God might want Northland to help establish. As he prayed, Joel sensed a clear answer from God: *One million.* Though he struggled with the feeling that this was an unreasonably large number, Joel could not deny his strong impression.

Coincidentally, at that same conference, Dan Lacich came across GMO's booth. They recognized the overlap of their visions and a new partnership was born. Networking together has created one of the most innovative movements in contemporary missions. As countless other churches catch the vision of networking with GMO and Northland to reach the nations, Joel's dream of planting a million "simple churches" around the world doesn't seem quite as unreasonable anymore. The revolutionary concept of online missions is transforming the congregation and broadening their understanding of ministry, according to Dan: "On the one hand, it will have an impact out there in the world. It does that — no doubt about it — but the change it makes in the congregation is amazing. Building confidence to share faith grows like crazy. It equips to do ministry in the real world by building confidence in a safe environment. We are seeing enthusiasm for ministry like never before. The way it is changing the online missionaries' worldviews is huge."

Back to the Future

What does the future hold? Only God knows. But it's obvious that the Surge of God's passion for the nations is going virtual and viral. Just talk to Lee Martin, a layman from Two Rivers Church in Knoxville, Tennessee. Lee is an entrepreneur, a professor, and the author of the book *Techonomics: Anticipating the Future.* He also happens to be an online missionary who, like Sarah, leads a small team from his church that is reaching the nations via the internet. In his book, Lee cites "Moore's Law," which says that every two years either the power of a computer doubles or its price drops in half. He also discusses the idea of "Metcalf's Law," which describes how internet connections grow exponentially — much faster than the simple *addition* of users.

What does all this mean for the nations? Walt Wilson describes the potential impact these new technologies can have on our outreach efforts: "We now see the day when everyone will own or have access to a very inexpensive handheld smart thing — one that speaks, shows movies, takes pictures, plays music, connects to other people, and tells him or her the story of Jesus. Apple's iPhone technology is a glimpse into the future. It is not a phone; it is a network computer. Like dawn coming over the horizon, we are now close enough to see the day when we will tell every man, woman, and child on earth the story of Jesus. The fields are white … the days are short … we have the technology."[9]

Some of this technology is being driven forward by a movement known as the O3b Initiative (O3b stands for "other 3 billion"), a worldwide plan to provide cheap high-speed web access via satellite to the three billion people on earth who are not yet online. If efforts like O3b succeed, it may not be long before the entire world will be linked wirelessly — largely thanks to secular market forces. If churches are ready to work together, we can take advantage of these global movements and ensure that everyone on earth has multiple opportunities to hear and respond to the message about Jesus.

In this e-Surge, billions will be given the opportunity to accept Christ, grow in their faith, and become connected to Christian ministries across the globe. The overall strategy is to move people and people groups from isolation to connection with one another, and to move beyond the simple relaying of information and toward the transformation that is possible through increased connectivity and relationship with other believers. But there is a lot of work still to be done — and innovative young people will be needed to help guide the church into this highly connected world. Existing ministry resources will need to be translated into English, Chinese, Japanese, Spanish, German, French, Korean, Italian, Portuguese, Dutch, Arabic, and Russian — the key languages spoken by 85 percent of all people on the internet. Seekers will be sorted by zip codes and regional codes so that emails can be routed to online missionaries who might be living near them. The goal is that those who are seeking God in the virtual world will be able, when ready, to make the transition from bits back to atoms and become part of the body of Christ in the physical world.

Walt Wilson's words echo the ancient mandate of the Great Commission as he proclaims the direction we are headed in the information age: "It is our calling and vision to reach every man, woman, and child on earth. As we look at the future, we view technology not as a snapshot but as a rapidly moving video running at super speed. We see newly developing silicon chip sets making new things possible almost monthly. We see acceleration here in Silicon Valley that has not been seen before. Knowledge, capacity, and scale are exploding."

> We must not be dazzled by the wonders of technology and think that the need for mighty intercessory prayer is obviated, the need for the cross and suffering nullified, or the value of real-life acculturation and incarnation of expatriate missionaries within the culture lessened. Technology lessens our sole dependence on physical nearness and direct personal contacts, but it does not lessen its value.
>
> — Patrick Johnstone

If you've been looking for a jumping-off spot, a place to dive into the river or just dip your feet in the water and get a sense of the flow of the Surge, then this may be your starting point. The world of bits is an economical and extremely effective place for many people to get started in the Surge. Ministries like GMO are creating the infrastructure (GlobalMediaOutreach.com), and hundreds of churches are taking the plunge. Or you can personalize your church's outreach by organizing a volunteer team to turn your church's website into an effective outreach tool. With a little prayer and some brainstorming, who knows where God might take you? Home fellowships, coffee houses, youth group rooms, Sunday school classrooms — all have the potential to be transformed into real-time, world-reaching venues that touch the nations through keyboards and computer screens. Consider timing the launch of your new ministry to coincide with Internet Evangelism Day (the last Sunday of April) as a way of gaining some momentum and connecting with the larger global movement. Another first step might be to prayerfully consider whether your church could become a "platoon" of online missionaries.

The virtual fields are white and ready for the harvest. We believe that this is more than a passing fad — it's a new global movement. The Surge is headed in a new direction, and it's accelerating exponentially. Real souls are being saved, real connections are being made, and real needs are being met by the Savior working through his church in virtual meeting places.

Each of us has the opportunity to reach some of the farthest corners of the globe and give a drink to a thirsty person looking for the refreshing water of the gospel, all without ever leaving home. In many ways, this change is nothing short of a miracle. For those of us who still think of missions as pith helmets and Bibles packed in caskets, this virtual flood represents the unthinkable.

> O Breath of Life, come sweeping through us,
> Revive Thy church with life and pow'r:
> O Breath of Life, come, cleanse, renew us
> And fit Thy church to meet this hour. . . .
>
> Revive us, Lord! Is zeal abating
> While harvest fields are vast and white?
> Revive us, Lord, the world is waiting,
> Equip Thy church to spread the Light.
> — Hymn by Bessie Porter Head (1905)

Who would have thought that getting caught in the Surge might be only a few mouse clicks away?

A Church in the Surge
Reaching the Nations through the Internet
Forestville Baptist Church
Greenville, South Carolina
www.forestville.org

Rob Jackson was the vice president of campus life at Liberty University (which has one of the largest online Christian education programs on the planet) when he was tasked to build a spiritual infrastructure for distance learning. During his research, he came across GMO and the idea of becoming an online missionary. "I was skeptical at first," he said. "But then I thought, *If this is true; if there's even a chance that this might work, I want to become a part.*" In his first month as an online missionary, it became clear that these were real people making real decisions for Jesus. That was three years ago, and he describes the ongoing experience with one word: "Phenomenal." Today he is the senior pastor at Forestville Baptist Church, and he is still an online missionary.

"This may be the most fruitful thing I ever do. I have personally had the opportunity to minister to eight thousand people in 140-plus countries. Recently I was able to respond to two seekers from four tiny islands near Tahiti. They are considered one of the top five most isolated corners of the world. One day I was corresponding with a Pakistani as I watched battles with Taliban take place on CNN. He was in the same region."

Forestville has about twelve hundred regular attendees, and about eighty of them are online missionaries. "I encourage families to do it once a week, and it transforms them. The personal life-transformation in the congregation is just phenomenal. We have one blind woman who lost her long-term memory and was wrestling with depression and purpose in her life. Joy returned to her as she began to participate in this life-giving movement. Some Sundays, I ask the congregation where we have ministered in the past week. The answers come back from every corner of the globe: Ethiopia, Kyrgyzstan, Venezuela ..."

Not only has Forestville's online ministry been effective worldwide, but also the training and experience they've received has made the congregation more effective in ministering to their own communities. "As they help people, they also learn themselves, and it takes away the fear factor about sharing their faith in general."

Forestville is just one of thousands of medium-sized churches in North America, but God is using them as individuals and as a body to be "living temples" to the nations of the world via the internet.

"My seven-year-old son sits on my lap at the computer with a globe, so we can pinpoint and pray for the people we are emailing. It's just phenomenal."

Wondering where to start? Feeling energized but alone? Jump in at *www. GetInTheSurge.com*, where you will find resources and links for pastors, small groups, and mission committees.

Chapter 5

Local Flooding

The Nations in the Neighborhood

> Students and recent immigrants come to the US with specific educational and career goals and plans; most of them are unaware of a personal divine plan from God.
> — *Douglas Shaw, president of International Students, Inc.*

Laughter rose into the dusty sky. Heavily accented words such as *wickets*, *creases*, and *pitch* filled the air as my fifteen-year-old son Cameron struggled to catch on to the game. We were half a world away from home, playing cricket with our church planting partners in India. Cam being highly athletic, his interest grew, and after an hour he had the basics down. That afternoon was one of the simple highlights of our trip, and Cameron brought the memory back to Dallas, where he coerced his brother and sister into a makeshift game in front of our house. Three sticks broken from the branches of trees behind the house were fashioned into a wicket; a pool flotation kickboard made an adequate bat. Laugher again filled the air as they played in the street.

Then a car rolled to a stop and an Indian man jumped out. "That wouldn't be the great game of cricket I see being played in my neighborhood, would it?" he exclaimed. We soon learned that he was from Bangalore, the first city we visited on our journey. We had just traveled halfway around the world to see his nation; he had moved to Texas with his family to find a better life ... and he lives a few houses down the street.

Before we knew it, he had invited Cameron to play on his cricket team ...

• • •

It was nine o'clock at night, and Todd was exhausted as he bungled down the aisle of the airplane in Phoenix, looking for his seat. It was the last leg of a long trip home from LA. Todd, my friend and fellow writer, was looking forward to drifting off in anonymous slumber as he made his way back to San Antonio, Texas. No such luck this time, though. As he neared his row, Todd took a deep breath — a darker-skinned man with a turban wrapped high on his head was sitting in the seat next to his.

The man was from New Delhi, and the melodious sparkle of his accent immediately melted Todd's selfish thoughts. For the next hour they talked about their families, about their countries, about politics, about their cultures ... about what it was like for this man to bring his Middle Eastern – looking family to the United States in early September 2001 (no joke!). The conversation freely flowed toward religion. The man belonged to an oppressed religious minority called the Sikh — one of the eight thousand unreached peoples scattered around the world. Interestingly enough, there is a Sikh temple not far from Todd's church in San Antonio. The temple is also home to a highly ecumenical multifaith organization. The organization sponsors a multifaith camp where students from different religions can enter freely and can openly discuss their faith with one another. "Perhaps you will come and speak about Christianity someday, yes?"

• • •

Our daughter, Annika, attends a public middle school near our home. She can travel from one class to the next and not hear a word of English in the hallway. Where we live, Spanish is the language of choice. Our son is a minority in his high school, which, when the students file out at the end of each day, looks like a copy of the United Nations.

Something is happening right here in North America. The Surge — God's global movement to reach the nations with his message of love — has come to us. In fact, it's often right in our own neighborhood.

The World on the Doorstep

Cameron, Todd, Annika — none of these individuals would consider themselves missionaries in the traditional sense, yet each of them has had opportunities to share the love of Christ with people from different cultures, right in their own hometown. No longer do we need to go out searching for the Surge — in many circumstances, the Surge has found us! The unreached nations are now coming to our doorstep, and the people of the world are moving into our neighborhoods. America has always been a melting pot of Europeans, Africans, Asians, Hispanics, and other ethnic groups. In the last thirty years, a wave of massive urbanization and international commerce has turned our cities into rainbows of ethnic and religious diversity.

To some, this is seen (at least initially) as bad news. They see the influx of new, foreign faces as an imposition, a loss of influence. But if we are able to take a step back and begin to see the world as God sees it, we will recognize this as a remarkable opportunity to reach out and *literally* touch the nations that have moved within arm's length. Perhaps it's the German exchange student sitting next to you on the bus, or the Bengali woman with a head covering standing behind you in the grocery store, or the Vietnamese family who sleeps in the back room of their restaurant at night and serves some of the hottest food on the planet by day.

It's time for us to open our eyes and look at what is happening right in front of us. In many of our cities, in many of our suburbs, and even in many of our rural areas, God has done the hard work and brought the nations and the peoples to us. This is something that is happening *now*. No longer can we avoid the implications of the Great Commission by telling ourselves it's a job only for missionaries in far-off lands, somewhere "over there" where we are unlikely to ever travel. There are opportunities to reach the nations right where you live. God's passion is not linear and predictable. He doesn't always follow recognizable plans or one-size-fits-all strategies. He can use any situation and any means to spread the word about his love — even bringing the people he wants us to reach right to us!

Consider what God did in Acts 8. Godly, brokenhearted men had just buried the stone-shattered body of Stephen. The servant of the Pharisee leaders, Saul, was on a rampage to destroy the church, going house to house and dragging Christ sympathizers out and throwing them into jail. The fledgling Christian church was bruised and scattered; it appeared that this small movement was nearing extinction. But as we look back now, we see that this was really just the beginning of a global movement that would change the course of history. "Those who had been scattered preached the word wherever they went. Philip went down to a city in Samaria and proclaimed the Christ there" (vv. 4 – 5). God began to move in power among the people, with signs, healings, and demonic deliverances. A powerful sorcerer named Simon believed and was baptized. Peter and John were called in for quality control, and the Holy Spirit began to spread through the small groups of Christ followers through the laying on of their hands. As John and Peter made their way back to Jerusalem, God used them to spread the word through many villages among the Samaritan people group. And what about Philip? An angel of the Lord told him to head south on a desert road that goes from Jerusalem to Gaza:

> So he started out, and on his way he met an Ethiopian eunuch, an important official in charge of all the treasury of Candace, queen of the Ethiopians. This man had gone to Jerusalem to worship, and on his way home was sitting in his chariot reading the book of Isaiah the prophet. The Spirit told Philip, "Go to that chariot and stay near it."
>
> Then Philip ran up to the chariot and heard the man reading Isaiah the prophet. "Do you understand what you are reading?" Philip asked.
>
> "How can I," he said, "unless someone explains it to me?"
> — *Acts 8:27 – 31*

Take another look at this short passage, because it's a beautiful picture of how God works behind the scenes to bring both the seeker and the speaker together. As we consider the context, we see that God used the persecution of the church to send Philip into Samaria. Then he used secular commerce to bring Ethiopia to Philip! *And God is doing the same thing today.* Yes, God is still sending his people out, and he will continue to call faithful men and women to leave their families and homes and go out to reach the nations with the gospel. But God has more than one strategy. He has brought the nations of the world, and the unreached people groups who have never heard the gospel message, to us. They have come looking for a second chance at life; God has brought them here to give them an opportunity to hear the words that give eternal life. In most cases, these individuals are unlikely to darken the doors of our churches, yet they live in our neighborhoods, study in our educational institutions, and labor beside us in our workplaces. The harvest of the nations is literally all around us. Open your eyes and prayerfully begin to see the opportunities God is providing.

Home Delivery Available

People groups are typically insulated from one another by geography, culture, language, caste, and religion. Going out to the nations is never simple or easy (even though it is always worth it). For traditional missionaries, breaking through the insulation of another culture requires time, training, language learning, financial support, and significant investments of logistical effort. Most missionary families prepare for *years* before getting on an airplane, and in many cases upward of one hundred thousand dollars per year is required to keep them on the field.

Once these individuals and families arrive, many find themselves in a challenging political climate. It's a sad reality we must honestly face, but Americans are not always very popular with people in other nations. Some of them fear us. Many of them distrust us. Eighty-three countries have *officially* closed their borders to American Christian missionaries. Think about that for a moment. That's almost half the countries on the planet! Some of these nations will no longer listen to our message because they disagree with the policy decisions of the United States government. Some parts of the Muslim world have given us the label "occupiers" or "new crusaders." My point is not to agree or disagree with what our country is doing; I'm simply saying that we must face the reality that many people will reject us — and what we have to say — simply because we carry an American passport.

Taking Christ to the nations by traveling to foreign lands has always been a risky business. It was risky to travel in the first century, and travel has continued to pose significant danger for followers of Christ down through the centuries. While many areas welcome missionaries and the work they do, other parts of the world are engaged in tracking down and discouraging missionaries from accomplishing their work. Revolutions, hijackings, kidnappings, beatings, sickness — the ends of the earth often shatter our Western illusions of safety and security. Terrorists, extremists, gangs, and even governments pose great physical danger to missionaries on a daily basis. Many missionaries seek safety behind the walls of mission compounds; others take risks and return home traumatized.

Yes, it's tough to work in certain fields. And it's always hard to live on the mission field, regardless of where we are called. It's even tough coming home, once you've been gone for a while. But while going out to serve is very costly, both financially and emotionally, God has now "home delivered" the nations right to our front door. Many of the very people we are trying to reach with God's love have already paid all the prices for us. They have left their families behind; they have paid their own travel and living expenses; they are learning our language; they are overcoming cultural barriers and enduring prejudice from others. Why? Well, since we know God is in control, we know that ultimately it's all so we can share Christ with them (though they may not know that quite yet!).

Even more, those who come to the United States are often the best and brightest of their home culture. Unlike the immigrant ancestors of past movements (who were mostly social, political, and religious outcasts), many of those who are coming here now are some of the most intelligent and influential future leaders on the planet.

Immigrants

Each year for the last five years, over one million legal immigrants have made the United States their home. Last year that included six hundred from Kyrgyzstan, sixty-three thousand from India, nine thousand from Egypt, and eighty thousand from China. Another one hundred and sixty thousand entered under refugee status, including thirty-four hundred from Uzbekistan, two thousand from Cameroon, and another twenty-one thousand from China.

Many of them do their best to integrate into the mainstream of American culture. Others tend to cluster together with their own people group. The people groups themselves tend to cluster with other people groups in certain areas of a city. In east San Diego, for example, thirteen different "nations" can be identified within a two-mile radius.

Many of these communities are hidden by patterns of segregation that keep everyone on their own side of the tracks. But even if we don't always recognize the strangers in our midst, they are still there.

How can we prayerfully and faithfully reach out to these nations among us? Priority one is being secure in who we are in Christ — secure enough to break the expected patterns and practices that often accompany "missions." For most of us, an oppressive sense of obligation often accompanies the word *missions* — particularly if we understand it only in the traditional evangelical sense. When we become fixated on a narrow understanding of what missions is supposed to look like somewhere else, and try to recreate that experience in our own context, our creativity can get clogged up like a logjam on a river. We can easily grow distracted and discouraged.

Consider the experience of Alamo City Christian Fellowship. Alamo City was a church born out of a very difficult and high-profile church split. David Walker was the senior pastor of one of the most respected and prominent churches in his region. He had a heart to open the church doors to everyone, people from every social class and cultural background. It was a conviction that didn't sit well with the existing coat-and-tie pew culture of the church. Inevitably, a divisive battle over the purpose and future direction of the church ensued. In the end, even David's closest friends voted to terminate him from his position so he could start over with a fresh vision. David left the church and started Alamo City Christian Fellowship in an abandoned mall on the other side of town. They started with a massive amount of space in a former big-box retail store, and they were ready for something, but they weren't quite sure what it was going to look like. This new congregation began praying and thinking creatively about ways that God might want to use them to reach out to the community around them.

Today Alamo City is home to six different communities of believers worshiping under one roof. The facility houses a congregation of former communists from Vietnam, Laos, and Thailand. They host a gathering of ostracized Messianic Jews, along with two Spanish-speaking congregations and two African American churches. They even provide free office space for Hobbs House of Hope, a Kenyan orphanage ministry.

The building has become a hub of international activity. And things often get messy. An old proverb says, "Where there is no oxen the manger is clean, but much increase comes to the strength of the ox." Alamo City Christian Fellowship now has a front-row seat to see God reach the nations in their midst — even inside their own building! In many ways, the Alamo City church facility has become what the original temple was intended to be: a house of prayer and worship for the nations.

Cultural/Religious Associations

Imagine that groups of unreached Bengali, Iranian, or Pakistani nationals and recent immigrants are inviting you to become a part of their "club." Now don't just imagine it — experience it! All across the nation, immigrants, refugees, and students are organizing cultural associations with the intent of promoting fellowship, preserving native customs, and providing platforms for effective integration and survival in America. The vast majority of these organizations are open to Americans who are willing to come and listen, share in their struggles, celebrate their victories, and become helping hands to those who in many cases come to this country with nothing but the shirts on their backs.

The Federation of Turkish American Associations, Inc., for example, is an umbrella organization for over forty-three Turkish American Associations (TAA), each with numerous chapters. Found in nearly every major city in the United States, they are established to give support to Turkish students and residents and to build bridges of understanding with American neighbors. Stop and consider that for a moment: *The fifty-five million Turks represent one of the largest unreached people groups on the planet, and those who are here in America want you to come to their gatherings.* Fifteen years ago, the number of Turkish believers was about one in a million (literally). A tremendous amount of sweat, tears, and blood has been shed in this nation (including the recent brutal murders of three men who helped run a Christian bookstore). Hundreds of Turks are now responding to the gospel, and few people would question the expenditure of effort to reach this strategic nation. But at the same time, as we consider how God would have us reach this unreached country, wouldn't it make sense to patiently, selflessly, and authentically love the Turks whom God has delivered right to our door?

Cultural associations may not always be obvious or easy to locate. You may have to do a little snooping around to find them in your area, but they are there, meeting in makeshift mosques and temples, gathering to celebrate holidays and festivals. Let me encourage you to begin by asking God to open your eyes to see the opportunities behind this open door. Last week at our church, we had an Indian social gathering for a group from our community. They used our building for a four-hour talent show. Nothing religious or "Hindu" happened during that time: just some good fun and laughter, and a deep appreciation for a Christian church that was willing to open its doors and share the love of Christ in a natural way.

Migrant/Seasonal Workers

You may not know this, but many of our national parks and monuments are largely staffed by young people from other countries. Often, they come to the United States for a summer, hoping to make a few bucks and experience American culture, but most of them find themselves crammed in dorms and working long hours at menial jobs. Foreign workers are also part of the economic model that keeps the Club Med / cruise line industry afloat. I'm not sure that I can in good conscience endorse a mission strategy that involves taking regular vacations to the Bahamas or Glacier National Park, but even if you go just one time, you'll find yourself shoulder to shoulder with dozens of young people of different nationalities and cultural backgrounds.

There are plenty of ways a church can get involved in reaching these workers. What if your church's college students strategically decided to enter this workforce with the intention of building friendships and sharing Christ with their coworkers? Is it possible to reach the nations, get paid for it, and work on your suntan all at once? Sounds too good to be true, I know. Another idea, for those who aren't looking to start a new career, is to locate the living quarters for the internationals who work at your nearest national park or monument and invite them to your house, offering them a home-cooked meal and a chance to see a real, live American family in action.

In addition to sharing the gospel with seasonally employed college students, there are also opportunities to reach out to migrant workers and illegal aliens. Now, I know this is a *political* hot potato, but once we dial down to the issue on a *personal* level, the situation is a bit less confusing. Many of these people are parents desperately searching for a way to provide for their families, willing to risk life and limb to find work and a meal. A church in Tempe, Arizona, once discovered a cluster of migrant workers living down by the local river. Fearing deportation, these families were cut off from everyone — except from those who exploited them for profit. One child at the camp had died because of the lack of basic nutrition and health care; her body had been tearfully buried in a makeshift grave by the water. Carefully and cautiously, a family from the church approached them — like someone trying to help a wounded animal — and they were able to reach out to them through intentional acts of kindness in Jesus' name before the group moved on to find additional work. There were no earthshaking revivals or mass conversions to report. But the church was able to see Jesus working through their love for these workers, as his body reached out to "the least of these."

Foreign Exchange Students

At Bent Tree, we have a tradition of putting roses on the stage each time someone in our church shares Christ with a seeker and they respond and find new life in Christ. We recently had someone put a yellow rose on the stage, representing a teenager who had trusted Christ. Curious, I asked one of my staff members for a little background, and I learned that this rose represented an exchange student from Switzerland. Her American "family" had shared Christ with her during her time in the States, and she had come to know the love of Christ through them. I was particularly excited to hear that this was the *seventh* exchange student to stay in their home over the years — and five of them had come to accept Christ!

These are just a few examples of what God is doing through the Surge. I hope you are beginning to recognize a surprising reality: *God is delivering the world to your door.* Being a missionary is no longer limited to traveling halfway around the world. You can be a missionary by inviting a foreign student into your home, extending the gift of hospitality, and asking them to live with you for a while. Dozens of agencies are ready and eager to help you make this a reality. By shopping around and exploring different options, you can easily find students from every country on the globe — many of them from unreached people groups — who are ready to stay with you, who *want* to come to your home.

The Student Exchange Alliance, a growing, secular student exchange program, can match your family with students from the unreached nations of Azerbaijan, Taiwan, and Nepal (and sixty other countries, many of which have fewer than 3 percent Christians). According to their website, host families enjoy these benefits:

- "An opportunity for our family to help guide wonderful young people"
- "A different insight into what defines American culture"
- "Appreciation and pride in our country"
- "The opportunity for our children to experience something unique, and now they have an international sister"
- "Friends to visit in all corners of the world"
- "A chance for our children to see the advantages and benefits of learning a foreign language"
- "An international experience that our children are able to refer to when applying to colleges"
- "The benefits of experiencing community service while working with a nonprofit organization"
- "The knowledge to overcome cultural boundaries and misconceptions of the world around us"

Some friends of ours have a son who is an avid soccer player. Last year they welcomed a young German boy, a gifted soccer player, to live with them while he attended high school and played on the school's team. Not only was this student exposed to an evangelical church for the first time in his life, but also their son was exposed to another culture and developed a close friendship with him, built around their common love for soccer.

Inviting students into your home has an additional benefit: it provides opportunities for casual and natural sharing of your faith through conversations and questions that arise. It's hard to believe that God can use something this simple to impact the nations for eternity.

What if several families from your church networked together to host a group of exchange students from around the globe for a school year? Imagine how much fun you would have, working together to reach the nations through the gift of hospitality.

International Students

The United States educates more foreign students than any other country in the world. Nearly *one-third* of all international students worldwide are enrolled in U.S. colleges and universities.[10] This means that over seven hundred thousand of the world's best and brightest researchers and scholars live within minutes of a local church — and it may be *your* local church. Many of these students belong to people groups in places where there is no Christian church.

While some of these students are quite poor, many of them come from the upper levels of their society. Some come from families and elite circles of power and influence, and many of these students are the future leaders of their countries. They represent a stratum of society that traditional missionaries often have a very difficult time penetrating on the field.

Contemplate this sampling of world leaders who studied in the United States:

Afghanistan	Hedayat Amin-Arsala	Vice President	Southern Illinois University
Japan	Masako Owada	Crown Princess	Belmont College Harvard University
Israel	Shimon Peres	Prime Minister (former)	New York University, Harvard
Egypt	Atef Muhammad Muhammad Ebid	Prime Minister	Illinois University
Norway	Haakon Magnus	Crown Prince	University of California – Berkeley
Saudi Arabia	Prince Saud Faisal	Minister of Foreign Affairs	Princeton University
Thailand	Thaksin Shinawatra-a	Prime Minister	Eastern Kentucky University Sam Houston State University

Consider the last name on the list a bit more closely. Yes, you read that correctly: the prime minister of Thailand spent a few years at Eastern Kentucky U., next door to the Blue Grass Army Depot in Richmond, Kentucky. Did a local church welcome and serve him during his time in Kentucky? I don't know. But the next prime minister might be in the dorms down the road from your church. If you go to *www.educationusa.state.gov* and look under "information for U.S. institutions," you will find "International Students Yesterday — Foreign Leaders Today." It's an impressive list of names.

Are you beginning to get the picture? Living in America, far away from their friends, family, and the familiarity of their own culture, international students experience high levels of loneliness and isolation. Churches have a unique opportunity to serve these students with the love of Jesus, to bless them with kindness and minister to them with the message of God's grace. The field here is wide open, ready for harvest. Tragically, few churches and families are taking advantage of this unique opportunity. Only one out of five international university students will ever be invited into an American home.

What can you and your church do to get started? I have one simple word for you: *help.* Get started, not with a grand evangelistic strategy but by simply deciding to help them — with whatever they might need! Most likely, your local college or university has an entire office devoted to international students. And they need lots of help:

- Help finding homes for the holidays
- Help getting students to and from the airport
- Help planning cultural fairs and international festivals
- Help learning English
- Help finding a cheap, reliable car
- Help with taking sightseeing tours to local sites
- Help shopping and renting apartments
- Help identifying sincere host families who "adopt" a student or two during their stay
- Help with temporary housing

All it takes to get started is locating the international student office at your nearest college or university and walking in with a servant attitude. Tell them you and your family would like to be part of a meaningful cultural exchange with an international student and ask them, "What can I do to help?" If you enter the office with a genuine heart to help, you'll earn your place in their hearts — but first you need to check *your* heart.

Secular educational institutions are legitimately leery of religious organizations that are concerned only about conversions, people with a narrow agenda and little interest in genuinely loving students. If you are looking for spiritual brownie points to prove something to yourself or to God, or you need to fill an evangelistic quota, let me be quite clear here: don't get involved in international student ministry. You will likely do more damage than good. Recently one of my elders prayed at one of our meetings,

"Jesus, thank you for the privilege of spending our lives giving your love away." Begin by simply "giving his love away" to those who have never felt it before. And if you come across a situation where you think they are ready to receive the message of the gospel, then by all means jump in and tell them about God's love in Jesus.

International student ministry is a real blessing to those involved — and it can also be highly entertaining!

- Imagine taking a group of Japanese students to the monster truck races.
- Imagine a group of Ethiopians, who have never seen snow, laughing themselves to tears on your ski slopes.
- Imagine a Cambodian explaining to you, his language partner, how he makes turtle soup from the critters he poaches from the city park.
- Imagine trying to explain the rules of baseball to your new friend from Mongolia. "You get three strikes, four balls, and three outs ... After three outs, the team that was in goes out and the team that was out comes in, then ..."
- Imagine the tear in your eye when your Romanian "daughter" tells you she is engaged to a wonderful guy, beaming as she says that "he swept my feet off."

In case you are wondering, yes, these are all actual experiences. Who said reaching the nations can't be fun? The commitments you make in this ministry may be simple and short-lived or deep and lifelong. Rick was a mobile mechanic in Phoenix. He helped international students by simply donating some of his time and expertise to helping fix their cars and change the oil in them. Diane, on the other hand, is a nurse, a wife, and the mother of three boys. She has taken a young Japanese student under her wing, treating her as if she were her own daughter.

If international student ministry becomes a strategic focus for your church, networking will help to increase your effectiveness.

Parachurch ministries such as InterVarsity, Campus Crusade, and the Baptist Student Union may already have established ministries that have done all the groundwork for you. When churches come in from the outside offering to help, it's like a breath of fresh air that invigorates everyone involved.

Are you feeling overwhelmed by all these possibilities? Let me encourage you to rest easy for now. The goal of this book is not to make you feel guilty or overwhelmed. Begin by praying. Think. Listen. God will lead the way forward, God will provide the opportunities, and God will do this through you if he chooses. You don't have to do it yourself or try to reinvent the wheel. Others have gone before you, and there are leaders with passionate excellence and decades of experience working with international students who are actively seeking to network with local churches.

One of these organizations is International Students, Inc. This wonderful ministry has been reaching out to international students for more than fifty years, and they understand the vital synergy they share with the local church. Our church has been networking with ISI in various capacities for a long time. ISI is serious about networking with local churches, and they recently mailed out letters to twenty thousand churches nationwide, inviting them to get involved in international student ministry. If you and your church are interested in finding out more about this unique opportunity, *www.isionline.org* is a good place to get started.

Immigrants and refugees, migrant and seasonal workers, exchange programs and international students: *Where* in the world has God placed you already? *Who* in the world has he brought to your doorstep? Open your eyes; the harvest surrounds you! Let Christ live in you, and then watch him begin to move through you to love the nations in the neighborhood.

A Church in the Surge
Reaching the Nations ... from the Middle of Nowhere

Rimrock Evangelical Free Church
Rapid City, South Dakota
www.rimrockchurch.com

Drive through the vast open spaces of the upper Midwest and you're bound to find yourself on I-90, the only interstate highway in South Dakota. Take I-90 west and you'll find yourself in Rapid City, a town of 65,000 (75,000 if you include a nearby air force base — and 175,000 if you include the prairie dogs). Rapid City is the largest "city" within a 350-mile radius.

Though it would seem like an unlikely place for a local church to get involved in the Surge, that's exactly what's happening. Home to two small colleges (South Dakota School of Mines and Technology and National American University), this simple community is a town to which God has brought the world. International Students, Inc., and Rimrock Church are there to greet it.

"I'd never try to list everyone who has helped. I'm guessing forty to sixty families have been involved over the years," says associate pastor Mike Hays. "Anytime you get the congregation outside the walls of the church, we see that the church isn't about the walls — it's not about bringing people into the building; it's being used as his hands. We support ISI a little financially, but it's the usefulness of the gifts in our body that help the most. As a pastor, I've been involved to a certain extent, but by and large it's the congregation that has taken ownership."

Some families take students on ski trips. Others bring them along on hikes or holidays. When a medical clinic sold ISI a dilapidated office for one dollar, the church kicked in to help move it to a vacant lot between the two colleges and convert it into a vibrant living/meeting space. Suddenly everyone had something to do: carpenters, cooks, cleaners, language helpers, and small group discussion leaders.

Over the years, students representing seventy-six countries have come to the home for refuge, encouragement, fellowship, and worship. Many have discovered a relationship with the living God. For Rimrock Church, ISI is a place where those with the gifts of helps and hospitality can have an immediate and powerful impact as they answer Christ's call to reach the nations.

"My passion has always been to be a resource to the internationals," Pastor Mike says. "If we can train them and expose them here and then send them back, what better way to impact the world? And the blessing to our congregation is tremendous. We know about the Great Commission, but our partnership with ISI puts real faces to it — it becomes real, it becomes personal, and we see that it really matters. Just last week, a Chinese student was baptized in the river behind our church. When the congregation sees that, it changes them; it changes their worldview. *Theory* about the Great Commission becomes *reality*. We see that this is real; this is happening — and it's happening here and now, even in the middle of South Dakota."

Chapter 6

Reservoirs and Rivers

Money and the Mission

"The kingdom of heaven is near." Heal the sick, raise the
dead, cleanse those who have leprosy, drive out demons.
Freely you have received, freely give.

— *Jesus (Matt. 10:7 – 8)*

"Money, money, money." Just say the word and an emotional battle erupts in our souls. As Christians immersed in the world, we are continually bombarded by conflicting financial priorities. Dollars have the power to control our emotions and determine our choices, often leading us into an awkward and uncomfortable dance as we seek to justify our spending decisions. But money can also be used in ways that honor God, as we exercise wise stewardship of the resources he has entrusted to us.

Jesus spoke more about money than he did about hell, and the apostle Paul was certainly not afraid to share his God-inspired wisdom on this topic. Any discussion of God's plan to reach the nations will inevitably involve dollars and cents. You can't ignore the topic of money. The marriage of money and missions can be both terrifying and distracting, leading us into compromise, competition, guilt, and fear. Worse yet, it can erode our grand vision of the Surge, reducing it to small thinking and narrow priorities. Virtual missions are essentially free. Reaching nations in our neighborhoods costs almost nothing. From here on out, however, dollar signs are going to be attached to everything we dream about:

- The average price of a domestic summer mission: $427
- The price of a research trip to an unreached people group: $4,234
- Expenses for a family on the mission field for one year: $93,071
- Being truly free to launch ourselves into the Surge (and all of life) without financial constraints and with faithful abandon: priceless

Jesus came to seek and save the lost and to set captives free. Sometimes the truth hurts, but the truth is also what sets us free. Is it possible that God could use the Surge to set his people free financially? That sounds a lot like the God we see in the Scriptures.

Message from Macedonia

It's pretty hard for most of us to relate to the unique life of the first-century church. Two millennia distant and an ocean away, what these first believers experienced can often seem disconnected from ours in the modern age here in America. Tragically, this disconnect means that it's not easy to make the mental and spiritual connection we need to make with the life-giving and timeless truth they modeled. Yes, the early church has something to teach us about money, mission, and the Surge, and the differences between our lives and theirs, in the end, only make their lessons more powerful — and necessary.

The earliest Christians lived in a time when the middle class dwelt in stacked-stone houses, had dirt floors, built fires outside, had food when it was affordable, and spent their nights with everyone sleeping in a single room. They felt the cold chill of the winter months, and the sweltering heat of summer, blowing through the cracks in the wall. If you are like me, physical hardship is having my car break down, the sink back up, or the pizza delivery guy show up to my house fifteen minutes late. They saw earthquakes crumble their feeble structures, watched pests destroy their crops, and held their children as they died of disease — this was the *norm* for them. If these hardships were typical for those living in the first century, what would extreme hardship look like? I can't even begin to imagine. But that's the context in which Paul exhorts us in 2 Corinthians 8 to examine our hearts and our relationship with money: "Now, brothers, we want you to know about the grace that God has given the Macedonian churches. Out of the most *severe trial*, their overflowing joy and their *extreme poverty* welled up in rich generosity. For I testify that they gave as much as they were able, and even beyond their ability. Entirely on their own, they urgently pleaded with us for the privilege of sharing in this service to the saints. And they did not do as we expected, but they gave themselves first to the Lord and then to us in keeping with God's will" (vv. 1 – 5, emphasis added).

A "most severe trial," "extreme poverty" — considering the average and ordinary trials that people in Paul's time faced each and every day, this really puts things in fresh perspective, doesn't it? Just consider what the average believer lived through on a good day! These were people who had almost nothing to start with, and yet their "overflowing joy … welled up in rich generosity"? Don't let this just rush on by. Something really strange is going on here. In fact, these believers weren't even giving out of a sense of obligation or duty — they "pleaded with us for the privilege" of giving "beyond their ability." Every phrase of that passage paints a powerful picture, doesn't it? But there is even more to come. Just a few verses later, Paul makes an incredible statement, one that has been largely ignored by the modern Western church: "Our desire is not that others might be relieved while you are hard pressed, but that there might be equality. At the present time your plenty will supply what they need, so that in turn their plenty will supply what you need. Then there will be equality, as it is written: 'He who gathered much did not have too much, and he who gathered little did not have too little'" (2 Cor. 8:13 – 15).

In all our conversations about finances and the Surge, this text must inform and guide us. Paul is passionately calling churches to be generous and to put the Lord first in their hearts — not by bringing money in to spend on their own needs and priorities but by giving to those brothers in other parts of the world who are in need. Paul's simple goal is that the churches with more resources would give sacrificially so the less fortunate churches would be brought up and they would all be at the same level. Does that idea make you a bit uncomfortable? If you are starting to squirm a bit, know that I am too.

These passages are commonly used as proof texts to encourage *individuals* to give more generously to their church. But note carefully: the intended audience of Paul's instruction is the local church, collectively, not individuals in the church. Paul does encourage churches to faithfully support their pastors, but nowhere in the New Testament does Paul raise money for churches to spend on themselves. In fact, he is always raising money to meet needs in poorer parts of the world or for his own missionary endeavors (making requests for the latter somewhat begrudgingly). His primary challenge to the church is to *give* to other churches, not to *receive* from its own members: "You know the grace of our Lord Jesus Christ, that though he was rich, yet for your sakes he became poor, so that you through his poverty might become rich" (2 Cor. 8:9).

Do you see the sequence in Paul's thinking? The richer churches with greater resources voluntarily became poor so the poorer churches could become rich — the exact opposite of everything that the world and the credit card companies are trying to tell us. This is not some impractical, improbable, archaic theory.

This is the practical and powerful Word of God — and it applies to us today, just as much as it did to those early followers of Christ. The same Jesus is still doing the same work he did in the early church — changing hearts so we who are rich might voluntarily become poor, and in turn, those who are poor might become rich. Being a part of this amazing transaction can be one of the great joys of our life.

But are we anywhere near that reality? When it comes to money, is the local church a reservoir or is it a river? Are we damming up God's supplies for our own use, or are we letting them flow wildly and freely for his purposes?

Wealthy or Generous?

I found myself sitting in yet another church growth seminar. The presenter was a young "stewardship pastor" at a large church in our area. He was describing a group of churches that had been gathering under the name "the generous church community." PowerPoints flashed and we all oohed and aahed at the latest statistics — the most important of all being "average giving per unit per week" (a unit, it turned out, referred to people). Members of the generous church community were seeing two times the national average of giving each week, and (the kicker) the speaker shared that his church saw people giving approxi-

> Studies have shown that the richer we are, the smaller percentage of our income we give to the church and its mission.... Hard times, like persecution, often produce more personnel, more prayer, more power and more open purses than do easy times.
>
> — John Piper, *Let the Nations Be Glad!*

mately four times the national average per week. We peppered him with questions about how he and his staff were able to get their people to give so much. He explained that they have a fairly large staff dedicated solely to raising stewardship as a value, and their pastor has a passion for this topic and speaks on it constantly. It was all paying off, the speaker said, "because our church brought in almost fifty-seven million dollars last year."

> North American churchgoers gave more during the Depression (3.3 percent) than they have after a half-century of unprecedented prosperity (2.5 percent in 2004).
> — John Ronsvalle and Sylvia Ronsvalle, *The State of Church Giving through 2004*

Something stirred inside me. I wasn't sure what it was, but those words *brought in* helped define my internal angst. A question started swirling in my head: *How do we know if this is a generous church or simply a wealthy church?* A church composed of generous individuals does not always equal a generous church. As Jesus reminded us in the story of the widow's mite, generosity is not measured by what we "bring in" by large numbers and great wealth. Wouldn't a better barometer of church generosity be to measure how much a church *gave away* versus how much they kept for themselves?

I asked the speaker how much they save away, and the stewardship pastor admitted that he really didn't know.

Now, before we pull the sliver out of this young man's eye, we would do well to look ourselves in the mirror and see if the plank isn't just as obvious in our own. What are most Western, Bible-believing local fellowships (not just individuals) giving, and what are they keeping for their own uses and purposes? According to John and Sylvia Ronsvalle (who have been researching giving within the church for more than thirty years), congregations typically keep 97 percent of their income and distribute only about 3 percent to other churches and mission organizations.[11] I believe that these numbers speak for themselves. I am convinced that the evangelical church in America has become *wealthy* but not necessarily *generous* — and perhaps this is one of the core reasons why we have become stuck in those desert places, far from the life-giving flow of the Surge.

The church is designed by God to be a river of his riches, not a reservoir. The truth that it is more blessed to give than to receive is not just for individual believers; it's for the entire church. Sadly, the statistics tell us that the church in America isn't even a reservoir (which retains excess for use downstream). It's become more like the Dead Sea — stagnant and stinking, a place where the flow terminates rather than continuing through to others.

The financial "doctrine" of our culture, exemplified by our government, propagated by Madison Avenue, and embraced by most, goes something like this: *You don't have to have the money now in order to buy something. Just charge it and pay for it when you make your money later.* As a nation, we have adhered to this doctrine by racking up massive amounts of government and consumer debt. Because we are so indebted to others, when the offering plate is passed around, why would anyone in their right mind give? Many people think to themselves, *I'll get my financial house in order, and then if I have anything left, I'll give.* That's the pattern of our culture. It's no wonder that our stewardship sermons tend to go in one ear and out the other.

> One of the reasons churches in North America have trouble guiding people about money is that the church's economy is built on consumerism. If churches see themselves as suppliers of religious goods and services and their congregants as consumers, then offerings are "payment."
>
> — Doug Pagitt

Still, this is just a minor problem compared with the pattern set by churches as a whole. You see, churches are no different than individuals. *Individuals are simply doing what the body is doing.*

Collectively, as a church, we have bought into the cultural mindset that taking care of our own needs (and wants and frivolous excess) takes priority. In many churches, the financial needs of the programs, the staff, and the facility come first, and if there is anything left over, then — maybe — it will be given to support missions somewhere. I believe this is a desperately grievous misunderstanding of the power, purpose, and sequence of biblical giving, and it's killing our churches.

In direct contrast to the Macedonian churches, who out of their extreme poverty gave more than they were able, we have fallen into an affluent pit. Out of our ridiculous excess we give as little as we can get away with. I was cut to the core by this reality recently when an African friend candidly told me, "When I came to America, I was stunned that you build houses for your cars. The houses that you built for your cars are nicer than the houses African humans live in."

Steps in the Right Direction

In the early nineties, our church, Bent Tree, was giving a very small percentage of our operating funds to world missions. Mission support was simply a line item in the church budget, something that was rarely discussed but always funded, right around the 3 percent mark. Our mission program consisted of supporting a handful of full-time missionaries. At the time, the church was struggling financially, so any conversation about giving more to missions wasn't high on the agenda.

With my pastor-of-a-mission-minded-church mentality, I started to quietly inquire about the process of setting the missions budget. I came to realize that our giving such a small amount of money to world missions was simply a reflection of our passions and priorities. We gave so little because this concern wasn't very high on the list of priorities of the church. Reaching the nations was seen as "one of the many things we give to" instead of a primary, apostolic calling. At the time, we were giving around thirty-five thousand dollars annually to support missions. When I shared that I was convinced that a one-million-dollar budget was in the future, there were audible snickers of disbelief. Some people even gasped, because our annual *operating* budget then was slightly more than a million dollars. By God's grace, the Spirit led us to make a number of important changes, the most significant of which was our transition to a Faith Promise system of giving.

In the Faith Promise system, three steps of faith are made during our annual missions festival:

1. Individuals promise, in faith, to give a certain amount in the coming year for reaching the nations. This amount is recorded on a card and placed in the offering basket. The cards are tallied, and the sum total becomes the mission budget for the year.
2. Bent Tree promises, by faith, to provide this amount to our missionaries and toward mission projects.
3. The missionary goes to the field, in faith, anticipating support from us for their work.

As the Spirit began working in the hearts of our people, we saw an immediate increase in our missions giving, and this giving continued to trend upward for well over a decade. Along with increased giving, additional energy and momentum were also generated. I believe that part of this increase in enthusiasm about missions came from giving people the freedom to determine how much they felt God was leading them to give, in keeping with the spirit of 2 Corinthians 9:7: "Each man should give what he has decided in his heart to give, not reluctantly or under compulsion, for God loves a cheerful giver." As a church, we simply let the needs and the opportunities be known, and let God's Spirit do the rest.

The congregation also gained greater confidence in the process as we carefully explained how our mission team would ensure that their sacrificial giving was making a difference and accomplishing kingdom work. Our mission department became something like a well-diversified mutual fund. Our team does all the legwork and the research and then reports back to the church, recommending the best collection of investments for the kingdom. This "mutual fund" diversification model has worked very well for us at Bent Tree, and there's no reason why you shouldn't consider it as a model for your own church — but let me add that there's no reason why you *have* to implement it either.

Local congregations are single cells within the greater body of Christ, which is made up of millions of communities of faith. Together the body will naturally diversify its giving, even if each single cell were to focus its generosity in a single direction! For all I know, God may be calling you and your congregation to giving in a way that is focused like a laser beam, releasing your financial resources for one or two strategic purposes.

The Faith Promise system and "mutual fund" approach is just one way to do all this, and it may go the way of the dinosaurs by the time this book is out of print. Still, even as methods change, the basic objective remains: keeping the worldwide scope of our calling in front of our people and giving them enough information to invest wisely in God's kingdom work.

Another Step over Dinner

I was sitting at dinner with my elders and Clive Calver, then president of World Relief, and I just knew what he was about to say. Or at least I thought I did. And to be honest, I was growing uncomfortable with where I knew the conversation was going. Bent Tree was still in the early stages of budgeting and raising money for a building expansion. And I knew the question that was coming: "How much are these new facilities going to cost you?" (Of all the questions to be asked by the president of a relief agency!) "Twenty-five million," I said with a gulp. (Pause in the conversation.) Clive, thankfully, was both thoughtful and wise, and certainly more gracious than my insecurities were willing to give him credit for. "Listen," he said, "buildings are expensive here — about ten times more expensive than they are in the developing world. Why don't you 'tithe' 10 percent of what you raise for yourselves and invest it in facilities around the globe? With just 10 percent, you will be able to 'gift facilities' of equal proportion."

It took only a moment for the seed of that idea to take root in our souls; there was just something *right* about it. I looked around the room, and the elders were all nodding in enthusiastic agreement. Then and there we decided that we would do it. And when we took the idea back to the congregation, they responded in force. The passion for giving was becoming contagious. Of course, it was fun to watch the construction of our new facilities, but in all honesty, our own building endeavors took second place to the joy we shared as we saw our blessing overflowing back to the nations.

God used the 10 percent tithe from our building project to create twelve additional ministry projects scattered around the world. The first project was in Thailand, a two-story building that houses training for Campus Crusade for Christ staffers during the week and a Thai church on the weekend. It cost $168,000 *total* (we had permits that cost almost that much on our Dallas facility!). After that came a similar facility on the outskirts of Siberia, where our partners are raising up church planters, and a center in central Africa, where young leaders are encouraged and taught how to lead churches ripped apart by genocide and AIDS. And these were just the beginning. It left us all wondering what would have happened if we had "tithed" 20 or 30 or 50 percent!

> One cannot help but wonder what the result would be if this mass of laypeople could be spiritually released from their servitude in the American success system and re-oriented to channel their major energies toward building the Kingdom of God.
>
> — David Bryant, *In the Gap*

One significant side effect of all this was that I began to see how Bent Tree's heart followed our dollars. Commonsense wisdom would tell you that our hearts are what determine where our money goes. But Matthew 6:21 says just the opposite: "Where your treasure is, there your heart will be also." I began to see the power of this truth having a practical effect on our congregation. Our

> Money builds and money destroys ... the downside is that insidious slide toward dependency on the part of the receiver. I have yet to see such a dependent relationship that I feel good about.
> — Phil Parshall

"tithe on the building" was greatly increasing our collective passion for what God is doing around the world! (As an aside, let me challenge you to test this truth for yourself. If your heart has yet to be sucked into God's passion for the nations, maybe you should throw your wallet into the Surge, that is, give some of your finances to a worthwhile mission project or ministry, and then get ready to find your heart eager to jump in after your wallet!)

Now, I'll be honest with you. Not everything has gone so smoothly. We've been supporting a leadership training seminary in India for quite a while. One spring, we thought it would be really fun to give each of the graduating pastors a motorcycle that they could use to travel between their churches. The next semester, we experienced a different kind of surge: a surge in enrollment! It seemed like every young buck in the community was now ready to devote his life to the gospel ... as long as it had wheels attached. It took a little while to straighten that one out. We were generous, but we had to learn how to give the gift wisely.

Thankfully, wisdom is available for those who are teachable. The church now has two thousand years of financial mistakes in our corporate files. Giving generously but without wisdom has led to a tremendous amount of misunderstanding, greed, dependency, and conflict on the field. Counselors, mentors, books, and PhD-level thinking in missions journals can help save us from making unnecessary, damaging decisions. In many situations, we must be willing to *not* give even though we might *feel* like we should. If you are interested in doing some additional research on this, let me encourage you to check out resources like *Evangelical Missions Quarterly* and the *Perspectives* reader. These have some interesting and helpful insights that can help you avoid the mistakes of those who have gone before you. Both of these resources should be on the shelf of every pastor in America.

So, is Bent Tree a *generous* church or just a *wealthy* church? I think the verdict is still out on that one, but I know that by God's grace we are taking steps in the right direction, seeking to become a truly generous church that gives to God's kingdom purposes.

A Percentage or a Person?

Let's get down to the nitty-gritty, the question everyone is asking: "How much do I need to give to the nations?" (Or maybe, if we are honest, we think of it this way: "How much can I keep for myself?") If all this could just be reduced to a formula, my flesh would gladly adhere to it and eagerly proclaim it. The legalist inside me is always searching for that simple solution, the magic percentage that will tell me how much I have to give and how much I can keep for myself. It's that proverbial line where I can stop feeling guilty and simply retreat into comfortable opulence. What number would you like me to propose? Ten percent? Twenty-five percent? Would you feel justified and righteous if you gave 50 percent or more to the work of reaching the nations?

There is no magic line, no concrete benchmark for us to meet or fulfill. Why? Because nothing in the Surge is static; everything is fluid. *The Surge is not about a percentage. It's about a personage.* Certainly, committees and boards may need to come up with a number to guide the formation of the budget, and the congregation will probably have to approve it. But that's not the important part. That's not really the point of all this. If we become consumed with the numbers, we easily forget our first love and can be led astray from the simplicity and purity of our faith. Everything in the Surge is motivated by saturating our lives in the wonder of God's grace and mercy and his generosity to us. Our generosity, our giving, is nothing more than a liberating submission, another opportunity for him to speak to us and live his life through us.

If you absolutely *must* have a number, I'm fairly certain that it's somewhere between 0 percent and 100 percent. That's not a cop-out or poor attempt at humor; it's an *opportunity* for you. We each have the option to trust God and walk with him so closely that he can give through us with hilarious abandon. We have the opportunity to be students of the Word and learn to honestly recognize the materialistic, preconceived justifications we bring to the text. We have the opportunity to let the Spirit show us the principles of Scripture that can become our financial creeds — and our emancipation proclamations from worldly, fleshly bondage. Giving generously to the work of reaching the nations can be a test of our faith. Are we willing to accept Scripture for what it says, taking the clear meaning and applying it to our lives?

"I tell you, do not worry about your life, what you will eat or drink.... Look at the birds.... See how the lilies of the field grow.... Do not worry.... But seek first [God's] kingdom and his righteousness, and all these things will be given to you as well. Therefore do not worry about tomorrow, for tomorrow will worry about itself. Each day has enough trouble of its own" (Matt. 6: 25 – 34). You may have memorized this passage from Matthew years ago and may even have taught on it several times. But try, for just a moment, to imagine how your life would be transformed if you truly believed that God was your provider and you didn't need to worry about tomorrow, because you knew that God would be there to meet your every need. Imagine the resources that would be unleashed in your life — and I don't just mean financially! Freedom from financial worry will lead to increased creativity as all your gifts, your skills, and your time are invested each day according to one simple criterion: seeking first God's kingdom. What would it be like if we, along with our families and our churches, were freed from the stranglehold of Western materialism? What if all our energy, creativity, and resources were unleashed with strategic abandon in the Surge? What could God do? Where would we go? How free we would be!

> Nothing before, nothing behind:
> The steps of faith
> Fall on this seeming void, and find
> The Rock beneath.
> — J. G. Whittier

The underlying question that guides the relationship between money and missions is really quite simple: do we or do we not trust that God will provide?

We cannot serve both God and mammon. The heart has room for only one master. While we all long to be free from financial concerns, time after time we buy into the lie that if we just had a little more (just a little more), then we would be okay, then we could be generous (ignoring the fact that we are already, relatively speaking, the wealthiest of churches and individuals on the planet). Have we not become the proverbial tamed elephant, staked to the ground with nothing but a thin rope around our ankles?

The thin rope that binds us is cut by trust; freedom comes by faith in God's ability to keep his promise to us. I think there is something profound and powerful about those Macedonians giving away more than they should have, only to find themselves richer than they could have ever believed. This is the work of the backward God that we follow, who makes lavish promises to churches who give generously: "God is able to make all grace abound to you, so that in all things at all times, having all that you need, you will abound in every good work. As it is written: 'He has scattered abroad his gifts to the poor; his righteousness endures forever.' Now he who supplies seed to the sower and bread for food will also supply and increase your store of seed and will enlarge the harvest of your righteousness" (2 Cor. 9:8 – 10).

Remember, it's not our people who are giving to world missions; it is the Lord giving through our people. He supplies it all. His heart is to scatter gifts abroad to the poor. Not only will we have all we need, but the work he has given us to accomplish in our specific locale will flourish too. This is not about barely surviving; this is a promise of thriving!

But God also promises to "increase your store of seed and ... enlarge the harvest of your righteousness." God will give us a larger role to play in his kingdom work if we show ourselves faithful to give generously as a body. As a church, we have seen this promise fulfilled beyond our expectations and hopes. Not only has the Lord given us a larger role to play in the world, but he has funded everything he has called us to do right here in our local ministries.

Living like this as an individual is an amazing joy, but when this kind of life is experienced as an entire body, the supernatural movement of the Spirit is a delight that is almost impossible to describe. God makes yet another thrilling promise to us in the very next verse: "You will be made rich in every way so that you can be generous on every occasion, and through us your generosity will result in thanksgiving to God" (2 Cor. 9:11).

> Let us see that we keep God before our eyes; that we walk in his ways and seek to please and glorify him in everything, great and small. Depend upon it, God's work, done God's way, will never lack God's supplies.
>
> — J. Hudson Taylor

We don't need to explain this verse away, no matter how much it has been abused by televangelists. God promises to bless generous churches with all kinds of wealth: spiritual wealth, unity, growth, impact, effectiveness, as well as material wealth. This is the ultimate win-win-win. God's kingdom grows, our poor brothers and sisters are blessed, and our home churches mature in faith as they are used by God. Why are we made rich in every way? So we can be a conduit for the Lord *on every occasion* to spread his generosity around the world. God does all of this so that we can experience the eternal joy of getting swept away in his surging passion for the nations. Why? So we can be increasingly free of the numbing tension of living with one foot in the world and one foot in the kingdom. Why? Because under all of this, it's not about a percentage; it's about a person who loved the world so much that he gave his only Son so that we can walk in dependent freedom and trusting intimacy here and now — in this life as well as the eternal one.

Missions has often been seen as an outward act, but as we have unpacked it in this chapter, we find that the Surge is primarily an issue of our inner faith — our willingness to trust God. Because of this, any application or action we endeavor to undertake needs to be preceded by careful, honest introspection. *O God, search our hearts and show us our ways. Reveal any hurtful ways in us and lead us in the everlasting ways.* A few questions may be helpful to honestly consider and take before God in prayer:

- God, how is worry about tomorrow influencing my decisions today?
- Do I see my church as an end in and of itself? Lord, are we a financial reservoir, or are we a river of resources — a tributary into surging passion of your expanding global kingdom?
- Am I a child of the fish-and-loaves Jesus who can multiply meager resources? Or am I a slave of mammon (money)?
- Father, have the vision and desires you have given me and our church been dammed up by fear and finances?
- Do I really believe you are my security and my hope? Lord, can I trust you enough to pursue dreams without dollar signs?

Repentance with a Little Attitude

The popular soft drink named Surge was introduced to the market during one of the high points of the dieting fad (which seems to reappear every other year). While everyone else was taking the sensible, conservative path, advertising that their product had only one calorie (and in my opinion, zero taste), the guys selling Surge were boldly proclaiming, "All the sugar and twice the caffeine!" While everyone else was playing it safe, these guys took a risk — and people went all for it. Surge was incredibly popular as a new drink for several years.

I believe that the same counterintuitive approach is needed when we think about the Surge of God's love for the nations. (Okay, so the analogy breaks down all over the place, but hang with me for a moment.) What I'm suggesting is that *this is not the season to be careful and cautious.* It's time for us, as leaders and followers of Christ, to abandon ourselves and seek God's purposes with "all of our faith and twice our resources." This is the season for the Spirit, and not our spreadsheets, to drive our visions and decisions. It's time to be free, to quit counting nickels and noses and immerse ourselves in the power of the Surge. I believe it's time to step up to the edge of what seems sensible and take one step farther. Fear and flesh will scream in opposition, begging us to return to the "safety" of the desert lands, but when steps of faith are taken, then taken again and again, faith and freedom will rule in our lives and in our churches once more.

Although the number is so small that it's hard to measure, most statisticians agree that less than half a percent of all Christian giving goes toward ministry to unreached peoples (that's 0.005, half a cent on the dollar). Some are discouraged by that number, but I think we can look at that number in a different light: *think of the potential for growth!* If we can just tweak that percentage a little, we can *easily* triple or quadruple the financial resources headed toward the most spiritually needy nations. Ron Blue notes that "the annual income of evangelical Christians in the United States alone is about three trillion per year — nearly half of the world's total Christian income. Eighty percent of the world's evangelical wealth is in North America — and the total represents more than enough to fund the fulfillment of the Great Commission."[12] Unquestionably, tremendous potential is being stored in the financial reservoirs of the Western church. The question is really quite simple: do we or do we not trust God enough to release it?

Maybe you've heard about the pastor who wanted to encourage his congregation to give generously to a building expansion. He had good news and bad news to share with them: "The good news is that we have all the money we need for our expansion!" Everyone cheered excitedly. Then he said, "The bad news is that it is still in your bank accounts."

As silly as it may sound, I'm encouraged to know that the resources are there. We need to rise up and rebel against the status quo. It's time to be free and radical in our giving. Not just for the sake of the nations but also for our own spiritual growth and maturity. I believe it is time for us to live again by faith, not in worldly wisdom at the expense of faith, or exercising poor stewardship at the expense of genuine wisdom, but with as much godly wisdom and as much faith as we are able to exercise by God's grace. What if God's command for us to give generously and faithfully is as much for *our* good as it is for the good of the lost people we are trying to reach?

Friends, it is time for us to be generous *and* full of faith. No matter what it costs, it is time to live in freedom.

The Surge is building on two thousand years of experience. Draw from the insight of seasoned experts who are leading with innovation at *www.GetInThe Surge.com.*

A Church in the Surge
Extravagant Generosity

Cornerstone Church
Simi Valley, California
www.cornerstonesimi.com

By all outward appearances, Cornerstone Church was surging. With three thousand members in his congregation and an exploding public-speaking ministry, Francis Chan was the envy of many a pastor. So he quit.

"We had reached 'the top' and it all seemed so, so empty. It was very self-centered. I was self-centered, and therefore the church was self-centered. We gave away very little of what we had, because we were only concerned about *us* growing. It actually made me nauseous when I realized what we had done and what we had become."

A season of soul searching included life-changing short-term mission trips to Uganda. Honestly asking the hard questions, Chan was forced to ponder what life would *really* be like if he'd *really* trusted Christ with his money, schedule, and relationships. He reentered the pastorate at Cornerstone with an entirely new paradigm: rather than trying to grow the church, they began to choose the sacrificial and passionate ways of Jesus outlined in the New Testament. The question became, "How can we give more of our lives away?"

"We had started with our personal budget. My salary fourteen years ago was thirty-six thousand dollars. We kept it the same even though the church budget is now in the millions. I have seen miracle after miracle as we watch God provide for our family of six."

In turn, Cornerstone's elders have been willing to make some radical financial decisions. They abandoned plans for a sixty-million-dollar building project to free up large chunks of money for impoverished, hurting people. Now they are planning on creating an outdoor sanctuary and amphitheater that the whole community can use.

"We have adopted the approach of demonstrating faith by giving extravagantly and dangerously. About a year and a half ago, we made an on-the-spot decision to give away half of our church's income to those outside the church. We are still giving away about 55 percent of what God is putting in the plate. I could tell stories all day about how we see God's supernatural hand at work each time we step out in faith. It blows my mind and makes me cry."

Although Cornerstone appears to be light-years ahead of many, Chan knows in his heart that this is a process — an ongoing journey of trust and faith.

"I think we're heading in the right direction, but there's still a lot more to do. Several years ago, I actually got sick to my stomach when reviewing our church's budget. Today I'm extremely excited about how our church has become a funnel for God's resources. None of it is ours anyway. It all comes from him. He is the only giver. We are just living the cliché that we can never out-give God. It's invigorating for the whole body, it's making a difference in the world, and it's an absolute blast."

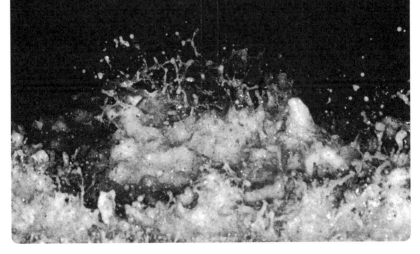

Chapter 7

Skinny-Dipping

Short-Term Exposure in the Surge

We in youth work have mistakenly assumed that the best way to relate to young people is to provide them with various forms of entertainment. For many of us, there is no end to the building of gymnasiums, the sponsoring of hayrides and the planning of parties. We would do better if we invited our young people to accept the challenge to heroically change the world.

— *Tony Campolo,* Youth and Missions

Ditto for adults.

— *Pete Briscoe*

I can't even remember his name, my brother in Christ, a man used by God to change the direction of my life. Born in Manila, Philippines, to a wealthy family, he was captured by Christ as a young man and sensed God calling him to plant a church in a tiny town on an island called Cebu. The pristine beauty of this seaside haven belied the undercurrent of an idolatrous and animistic religion that was leading the islanders to reject the message of God's grace. Their rejection was not unanimous, though. After five years of painstaking servanthood, my friend had discipled five dedicated followers of Jesus who regularly assembled in the fellowship of his tiny church.

One of the five church members was particularly noteworthy, a young boy, an orphan with a grotesque skin disease. In a scenario that recalled the rejection of lepers in biblical times, whenever this boy would enter the village, everyone would run away from him, screaming and cursing as they fled. The pastor had fought against the scrambling villagers and had made his way toward the boy, reaching out his hand of mercy. The boy accepted his kindness and came to know the Savior who would receive him, spots and all. He became a dedicated member of this tiny church and loved his pastor dearly.

Though this young pastor's acceptance of the boy led the villagers to reject him as well, he continued to offer himself to the community as a conduit of the Savior's love. All the while, the pastor had a secret prayer — one he placed before the Father's feet often, confident that one day God would grant his desire. Worlds away, on the other side of the planet, a nineteen-year-old sophomore was caught up in the midst of college life; my journey was about to intersect with the story of this young pastor on the island of Cebu.

You should know that I had two primary goals during my undergrad years: (1) to date every pretty blonde in my school (no small challenge in Minnesota!) and (2) to play as much basketball as possible. Full disclosure: it was this second goal that was the primary impetus behind my signing up for a summer mission trip with Sports Ambassadors (the results of the first goal are not the subject of this book, and honestly, won't be covered in any future publications either). I traveled to the Philippines with a team to play up to three basketball games each day, share the gospel, and encourage fellow believers. On one particular day, we drove our Jeep into Cebu, where the young pastor was continuing his ministry. Our custom was to immediately make contact with the local evangelical pastor so we could allow some of the goodwill directed at us to rub off on him. When we found this pastor, he was sitting alone in a thatched-roof home. We introduced ourselves, and I asked him if he would be willing to share the gospel at the game that night.

I'm not quite sure how to describe his expression. He was both joyful and terrified, resolutely committed and terribly frightened. "No," he replied, "I can't. Whenever I walk down our streets, the people throw rocks and batteries at me." He unveiled some AA-sized bruises to prove his point. "If I walk onto the court with you, some of you may get hurt by the flying objects." I insisted that we would be safe, that the towns we had previously played in were very welcoming and loved us. I had no doubt that his town would treat us with the same respect. He reluctantly agreed to work with us and told us he would arrive just before halftime.

As we were walking to the basketball court that evening, however, the usual excitement was missing. No welcoming crowds lined the street as we walked by. Instead a tiny woman approached us. No more than four feet tall and all alone, she walked straight to me and stopped directly in front of me. I smiled at her, and she started to talk. My smile quickly faded as I heard a deep male voice coming out of this old woman. In perfect English the voice said, "Leave this village now; you are not welcome here." Her eyes were glazed over with a vacant look, but her face suddenly contorted in anger and the voice grew threatening. My group leader grabbed my arm and pulled me away from her — my first (and to date only) encounter with a demon-possessed person. I had come to this side of the globe to help change the world, but the Evil One knew that God was about to radically alter *my* world, and this threat was a last-ditch effort to derail God's work in my heart. It didn't work.

Halftime arrived. We were leading the local teams by double figures and had won the crowd over with Harlem Globe Trotter–like antics. The whole town was there to watch the game, and they loved us! We stood in a semicircle at center court and sang a song to the crowd in their own language. They listened with rapt attention and cheered wildly as we belted out the last note. Then *he* walked out to center court. The crowd grew restless as the young pastor stood before them; their loathing of this precious man was palpable. Carefully he removed the microphone from the stand and began to speak. As he did, the crowd started to boo, hiss, and whistle, their protests growing to a crescendo that easily drowned out the words of the solitary speaker. I stood behind him with tears flowing down my face. He had warned me, but I had insisted; now he was being humiliated anew in front of the people he was giving his life to reach. He kept talking; they kept howling. As he led the town in the sinner's prayer, I glanced around to see them laughing, drinking, and spitting in his direction.

My head slumped as I returned to the bench to start the second half. I glanced up just enough to see the little Filipino feet of the rejected evangelist walking toward me. Sitting next to me, he placed his arm on my back. Starting my rehearsed apology, I slowly raised my eyes to meet his, and I noticed something remarkable: he was smiling from ear to ear! "Why are you smiling?" I asked. "You just got booed out of the place!" His response changed my life forever. My worldview shifted, my lifestyle realigned, my life calling cemented, and my definition of a pastor was established. "I am smiling," he said, "because I have been praying for five years for an opportunity to share Christ with my whole village, and tonight was the night!" The fact that they didn't hear a word was irrelevant to him. This was his dream, and God had granted it — and in doing so, struck deep into the heart of a young pastor's kid from the Midwest. That night, while the rest of my team slept around me, I lay on my bamboo mat and stared out the open window toward the stars:

Is this what it means to be a pastor, Lord? To sacrifice everything, to move to a place of your sending, to endure persecution, to preach anyway, and to find joy in living out the calling? Is this what it means to be a shepherd, Lord? To care for the ones you bring, no matter how few, to reach out to the rejected ones and love them too? Is this what it means to share the gospel, Jesus? To speak when prompted to do so, to surrender to the Spirit's power within and allow him to share good news with people who don't even want to hear it? Is this what it means to be a leader, God? To follow you as others follow me? Oh, Jesus, make me like him, I pray!

Skinny-Dipping in the Surge

Those moments, that night talking with the Lord, that experience on the Philippine basketball court — these were yet another defining moment for me. The opportunity to experience the faith of a young Filipino pastor firsthand, to see his passion for his people and meet him face-to-face — just sixty years ago that defining moment may not have been possible. While short-term mission trips are now a common part of the evangelical experience (particularly for youth and college students), that hasn't always been the case. The types of short-term mission trips we are familiar with today have been feasible only since the early 1960s, when air travel became an affordable means of transportation. Prior to that time, missionaries who wished to reach the unreached or support indigenous ministries had to commit themselves to years of service in a foreign land. Most short-term projects were domestically focused, and they offered minimal opportunity to encounter churches and ministries working among other cultures and nationalities. Today, short-term missions are something akin to skinny-dipping in the Surge — an opportunity to get a little wet and be exposed to the vast needs of the world

> If we could point NASA's Hubble space telescope back toward planet Earth, we would observe a steady flow of no less than 2 million people moving around God's globe every year on what has come to be called "short-term missions."
> — Roger Peterson, director of STEM

and the work of God's people in diverse cultures, while (hopefully) making an impact for God's kingdom.

Short-term missions usually reflect some sort of balance between two objectives: (1) legitimate service and (2) life change. Most people who pile in the van or jump on the bus or board an airplane go with the intention of serving others in some way.

They have a genuine desire to participate in something meaningful and helpful. Evangelism, children's ministry, medical ministry, labor-intensive projects, the training of leaders — you name it, and chances are it can be done while on a short-term mission trip.

But that's not the only reason (or the main reason) to go. Not long after short-term missions began growing in popularity, churches started recognizing an amazing side effect: in many cases, a short-term mission experience leads to some type of change in the lives of those who *go*. A recent study by the Barna Group shows that most of the people who embark on service adventures describe the trips as life-changing. In fact, three-quarters of trip-goers report that the experience changed their lives in some meaningful way.[13]

Something unique seems to happen when we go to serve somewhere outside the places we normally work and live. Perhaps it's simply stepping out of the proverbial comfort zone. Perhaps it's the intensity of the projects participants work on, often serving in new ways while stripped of the normal activities and cultural amenities that tend to insulate us from the real world. Perhaps it's the heightened awareness that comes from the investment of finances and time that participants are required to make to go on a trip. Or maybe it's a sign of the blessing that is unleashed as followers of Christ finally respond to their God-given calling to go and make disciples. Perhaps it's a little of each of these things. Regardless of the reason why life change occurs, churches have quickly recognized that short-term mission trips aren't just about serving others; they are a vehicle for helping facilitate spiritual growth in those who go.

All this has created an amazing phenomenon. Many trips are done on a shoestring budget, and youth groups in particular spend a lot of time sleeping on church floors to save money. If you could look down on our country from above during the summer months, you would likely witness a sea of buses and fifteen-passenger vans zigzagging across the continent. Many of these groups are traveling to communities where members from another local church have left to go minister somewhere else — and everybody sleeps on everybody else's floor as the people who serve come and go. Does it make sense logistically? Not always. From a practical, service perspective, it would make a lot more sense to just have everybody stay where they are. But that would ignore the additional benefits of short-term mission trips — most significant, their

> Mosaics are globally aware and cause-oriented. They relish risk, stimulation, and diverse experiences. And they are more sensitive to issues related to justice and poverty. Their craving to take journeys of service could fuel a resurgence of global engagement. Yet, the danger would be if leaders and organizations waste the Mosaic generation's readiness by simply allowing young adults to be mere "consumers of cause" — selling them a t-shirt or a wristband, instead of challenging them to life-shaping service projects.
>
> — David Kinnaman, the Barna Group

ability to catalyze a dramatic difference in the lives of those who go and in the lives of those they serve.

Barna's survey provided some additional snapshots of service trips:

- Most people take service trips outside the country; however, 33 percent of all mission trips were to locations in the United States.
- A person does not have to go far in order to grow personally through serving others. People who took domestic service trips reported the same degree of life-changing experiences as did those traveling abroad.
- The typical person who has been on a mission trip has taken two such journeys. Two percent of Americans are

service trip enthusiasts, having been on five or more such adventures.

In the past, church leaders were reluctant to admit that one of the reasons to go on a short-term mission trip was for us — for our own personal growth and maturity. But short-term trips have always had more than one purpose, even in the Scriptures. For example, take a look at the first New Testament short-term mission in Luke 10. Jesus had been engaged in teaching and training his disciples, equipping them for ministry through his words and through his example. Finally, the time came to kick them out of the nest and let them try it out for themselves. Jesus gave them clear instructions to follow and then sent them out. So what happened on this first short-term trip? What do we find when they returned home?

"The seventy-two returned with joy and said, 'Lord, even the demons submit to us in your name'" (Luke 10:17). Now, I'm certain the debriefing lasted longer than this single-sentence report, but I also find it interesting that the only recorded comment by those who went on the trip was about how the trip changed their perception of who *they* were. Of all the things they could have shared, they chose to focus on the amazing power that had been given to them through their association with Jesus. Note that Jesus didn't dismiss this; he built on it! He deemphasized what they had *done* for others and focused their attention on who they *were*: "However, do not rejoice that the spirits submit to you, but rejoice that your names are written in heaven" (Luke 10:20). The twofold purpose of their mission is clear. Jesus sent them to engage in legitimate service for others *and* have their lives personally changed.

Not a No-Brainer

Short-term mission trips seem to be a win-win scenario, beneficial for all involved. But is that always true? An honest assessment of short-term trips will recognize the benefits but acknowledge that not every trip has borne kingdom fruit or been conceived with wisdom. The jury is still out on this relatively new form of ministry, and a growing body of constructive criticism is challenging pastors and mission leaders to ask some tough questions about the practice of taking short-term trips.

An article in the *Christian Science Monitor* titled "Rise of Sunshine Samaritans: On a Mission or a Holiday?" raised concerns about the motives of short-term missionaries and challenged the idea that trips truly lead to life change: "Critics say an impoverished people, especially overseas, often end up pandering to cash-wielding, untrained missionaries who make a bad impression and don't make meaningful lifestyle changes upon return."[14]

JoAnn Van Engen of *Catapult Magazine* echoes the concerns of many critics, listing several problems with the practice of short-term trips:

1. "Short-term missions are expensive."
2. "Short-term mission groups almost always do work that could be done (and usually gets done better) by people of the country they visit."
3. "Short-term groups are also unable to do effective evangelism, which is the main goal of many groups."
4. "Short-term missions also require a great deal of time and coordination by their hosts."
5. "Short-term groups can also send the wrong message to third world people."[15]

While these concerns are not necessarily true for every short-term trip, her concerns suggest that we need to take a careful look at the practices and the purpose of our trips. In her article, Van Engen mentions a recent mission trip of eighteen students who spent their spring break in Honduras, painting an orphanage. The students raised twenty-five thousand dollars for the week-long trip. Keep in mind that the orphanage has a *total annual budget* of forty-five thousand dollars that pays for the staff salaries, covers building maintenance, and provides food and clothing for the children. Her point demands careful thought and reflection: "That money could have paid two Honduran painters who desperately needed the work, with enough left over to hire four new teachers, build a new dormitory, and provide each child with new clothes."[16] Furthermore, Van Engen points out that the team came down with a "let the North Americans do it" attitude, a mentality that often leaves nationals feeling frustrated and unappreciated.

To be clear, even with her criticisms, Van Engen doesn't believe that short-term missions should be abandoned. She is clear about the problem with these trips *and* their potential: "Third world people do not need more rich Christians coming to paint their churches and make them feel inadequate. They do need more humble people willing to share in their lives and struggles."[17]

In agreement with Van Engen is David Livermore, a scholar at Grand Rapids Theological Seminary and author of the book *Serving with Eyes Wide Open: Doing Short-Term Missions with Cultural Intelligence.* In a March 2007 interview with Calvin College, Livermore quotes several research studies that show the life-change impact of short-term mission trips to be negligible and short-lived, yet Livermore still believes that these trips can be worth the investment. That's good news, because we are investing a lot of effort, time, and money into these trips. Roger Peterson estimates that two billion dollars are spent on short-term projects every year. At their worst, short-term missions resemble a Club Med Christianity, something of a glorified vacation. Certainly, it is more than appropriate for us to question whether a sum this large is being invested responsibly in the kingdom. Are our priorities regarding short-term missionary work an accurate reflection and response to God's eternal passion for the nations?

Think before You Jump

When short-term mission trips are planned poorly or done for the wrong reasons, they expose both the host group and those going to numerous risks. We don't need to end the practice of short-term trips; we simply need to *think* before we jump. I'll be the first to admit that I'm a huge fan of short-term projects — *when they are done wisely.* With careful planning, short-term projects can be a revealing, rewarding, and, yes, life-changing experience. They can also be quite beneficial for the people we are going to serve, *as long as these projects are conducted with a mix of thoughtful, patient wisdom and Spirit-inspired enthusiasm.*

The website of the U.S. Standards of Excellence in Short-Term Mission *(www.STMstandards.org)* is an excellent place to look for resources and information to assist you in wisely leading and participating in short-term mission trips. You'll get advice from those who have made mistakes and have learned (the hard way) how to use a short-term project for maximum kingdom impact.

As I was writing this chapter, my daughter had just returned from a somewhat *different* short-term mission trip, a retreat with her youth group at our church. The idea behind this trip was for the group to focus their time serving in various homes here in Dallas, with a service project on Saturday morning and then some fun time the remainder of the day. That morning, they chose to serve at Sue's house. Sue is a member of our church. Shortly after her fourth child was born, her husband left her and the children (all under the age of six), and Sue was diagnosed with pervasive cancer. Intense chemotherapy, a radical surgery, and the responsibilities of single parenthood had taken their toll on her life, and her home was a complete mess. The girls on the "trip" descended on Sue's home, gutting out the garbage, sweeping the floors, and doing a thorough cleaning. Nine hours later (after skipping the fun part of the weekend), the girls walked out of a clean and organized home with joy-filled hearts and a realigned perspective. A young mother in great need had her home clean again, and several young women had their compassion stoked with the love of Jesus. As the girls were leaving, one of my daughter's friends walked over to the grateful young mom and said to her, "Hey, I'm a certified babysitter, and I would love to babysit your kids anytime you need me to … for free." That's what I would call a win-win! Short-term trips like this are worth their weight in gold.

To get started with the planning and preparation for a short-term mission trip, consider the following keys to a successful short-term project (gathered from multiple sources):

1. Ask the Hard Questions

- What is our true objective?
- Is this project highly strategic and a reflection of God's passion for the nations?
- Can the work we are doing be more effectively and efficiently performed by someone else? If so, why us?
- Is this trip truly an extension of God's grace working through us? (We aren't trying to prove anything by doing it in the flesh, are we?)
- Is this the best use of our time and resources? Are we maximizing the opportunity for life change *and* service?
- How far do we have to drive before the next rest stop?

2. Seriously Consider Focusing on Learning, Not Doing

In some situations, I suggest we stop thinking of short-term missions as *primarily* for the purpose of service and start thinking of them as opportunities to learn. There are exceptions, of course, where we need to just get in and achieve a specific objective (such as training people or building something), and legitimate service can also be a key aspect of the life-change process. But education can be equally important. Don't shy away from trips that are intended to teach people how to wisely steward the resources and influence God has given them for his global purposes. Groups like the Christian Commission for Development in Honduras are doing just that sort of thing, educating short-termers to have a long-term perspective on missions.

3. Submit to Local Leadership

Joel Carpenter, director of the Nagel Institute, says, "We assume that Christianity in the global South has a world of need, and that we are well supplied to meet those needs. The truth is that Christians and churches in Africa, Asia, and Latin America are quite resilient and resourceful. They often have been strengthened by God's help through tough times, so they have much more to offer us to meet our spiritual needs."

As Western Christians, we need to have a major attitude check here. Far too often, we are blind to our own sense of cultural and spiritual superiority. We tend to feel that we are God's gift to the nations, but that's never really been the case. *Christ is God's gift to the nations*, and we need to check our pride,

> They can fire vision, quicken prayer and catalyze commitment to more permanent engagement. But any short-term activity finds its greatest value when it exists, not for its own benefit, but as an integral part of a long-term process.
> — George Miley

and the sense that we have all the answers, at the door.

Early in your trip planning, set aside some time to carefully listen to the leaders of the communities you are planning to visit. These nationals are not your tour guides, so be sensitive with their time and try not to interfere with their ongoing ministry. So often, nationals feel they can't say no to our requests because of a cultural sense of obligation or because they feel an obligation due to our financial support. Don't even assume that they want or need you to come. Ask good questions and listen well.

4. Training, Preparation, and Follow-Up

Training of short-term participants and follow-up with them are crucial for a successful trip experience. If these aren't done, the teachable moments of the project may go unnoticed and can be quickly lost. Jason, a student who took a trip to Ecuador, articulated this beautifully a few months afterward: "You put all this time into it and then all of a sudden you're there and it's like, 'Wow we're really here, and we're really doing this!' ... and then I got back — right away I raced to my basketball game ... Later that night I thought, was I really there, two or three days ago? I was in Ecuador and it's just, yeah, it's like a movie, *almost* real. I can't believe it was real."[18]

One church requires a twelve-month commitment from anyone participating in its three-week short-term mission trips. This commitment includes six months of preparation and an additional six months after the trip for debriefing, reflection, and implementing long-term lifestyle changes. Regularly scheduled prayer in the months following the trip keeps mentoring relationships strong and keeps the lessons learned on the trip alive and growing. Strong mentoring relationships, therefore, are essential; *they are one of the most important aspects of an intense, short-term experience.*

Integrate good materials into your follow-up, materials that help walk participants through the process of making cognitive, faith-filled life changes. Remember, conscious decision-making is key for life change.

Young Adults Have Appetite for Service Trips

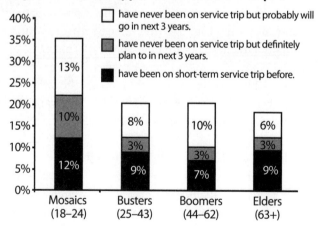

The Barna Group, "Despite Benefits, Few Americans Have Experienced Short-Term Mission Trips," October 6, 2008, *www.barna.org/donorscause-articles/22-despite-benefits-few-americans-have-experienced-short-term-mission-trips* (accessed July 2010).

Good for Kids; Great for Adults?

Lamenting how much energy youth workers put into entertaining their kids, Tony Campolo suggested, "We would do better if we invited our young people to accept the challenge to heroically change the world."[19] I wholeheartedly agree, but if that's true, why don't we extend the invitation to adults as well? I once saw a billboard that simply said, "Innertainment," followed by the name of a local church. Is that what our churches are really all about? Entertaining us? Building on what Campolo said about our youth, I believe we would do far better if we also invited our *adults* to accept a challenge to heroically change the world. There are real needs in our communities and among churches all over the world, and God is fully capable of working through us to make historic changes in this world. Short-term mission trips can be a significant factor in that invitation to accept the challenge.

> The label "life-changing" is pasted on many things, but the description fits most short-term service trips. Only one-quarter of those who have participated on such a trip said it was "just an experience," while a majority said it changed their life in some way. The most common areas of personal growth that people recall — even years later — include becoming more aware of other people's struggles (25%), learning more about poverty, justice, or the world (16%), increasing compassion (11%), deepening or enriching their faith (9%), broadening their spiritual understanding (9%), and boosting their financial generosity (5%). Others mentioned the experience helped them feel more fulfilled, become more grateful, develop new friends, and pray more.
>
> — George Barna

I believe that short-term missions can be even more effective in changing the lives of adults than in changing the lives of students. Adults typically have clearly structured worldviews and are able to assimilate new information and translate it directly into choices that lead to action. Adults also have had the time and experience needed to integrate their beliefs and may be better equipped to take concepts learned in one situation and apply them in another. Furthermore, adults in leadership positions can leverage a life-changing experience, often leading to ripple effects throughout their individual sphere of influence.

For example, I work with a church leadership that makes it possible for my entire family and me to get overseas to see the world and experience God's work firsthand. For years, our mission partners have been asking us to visit them on the field so I can get a better feel for their ministry and be better equipped to encourage those serving on the front lines. The church now budgets an amount for me to travel on an encouragement and support trip like this each summer. On one of these trips, my whole family traveled with me to visit the work we support in the Amazon River basin. I have also been able to take Cameron, my teenage son, to India to visit our partners there. What a blessing this has been! This summer, I'll be visiting our African partners with my daughter, Annika. Pastors and church leaders who want to lead others into the Surge really need to see the Surge and experience for themselves what God is doing in other churches around the world.

All that I'm saying comes down to this: Go. Get out into the world and experience the Surge with all your senses. Seeing God at work in these ways gets in your blood — it's infectious!

What If?

Over the past two decades, short-term mission trips have taken on a life of their own in the local church. Short-term mission trips, *carefully planned and done wisely*, can have a significant impact in the lives of those who go on them and can be a real blessing to those who are visited during them. With this in mind, let me ask you a simple but very practical question: what if you were to strategically realign your existing short-term mission efforts to match God's eternal passion for all peoples? In other words, what if you injected Surge-level thinking into every level of your short-term mission vision and leadership?

Let me explain what I mean. A common phrase in the missions movement today says we are "blessed to be a blessing to the nations." As true as that is, I also believe that the following is true: "By being a blessing to the nations, we are truly, truly blessed." Short-term mission efforts don't have to be merely a stepping-stone to reaching the nations. If we are willing to innovate and network, we will begin to see God's blessing poured out on the individuals who go *and* on the unreached people groups they visit. What if we really believed this? What would it look like if we pushed forward with a deep faith in God's blessing on our work?

What if you transformed your existing annual family camp or one of your church retreats into a virtual mission trip? Lots of resorts and camps now offer wireless internet, and you could simply have everyone bring along a laptop computer and encourage them to spend a couple of hours reaching out to thirsty souls around the globe through GMO. No doubt these "virtual mission blasts" would open up great discussions about apologetics, sharing your faith, and learning about the nations you are reaching!

What if you did your VBS this summer in conjunction with International Students, Inc., and invited internationals from the educational community to participate? What a unique way to bless the children of the nations among us! And I know your kids would be blessed to encounter diverse peoples and develop new friendships.

What if your youth group linked arms with a cultural association from an unreached people group? What if you worked *together* serving the homeless or recent immigrants in your area? Maybe you could brainstorm ways to improve the quality of life for the international, seasonal workers in your area.

What if ... I could keep going on and on, but I don't want to make too many specific suggestions here, for fear that you'll become limited to one of these ideas and fail to explore the ways in which your church is uniquely positioned and uniquely gifted. Think outside the box and ask the hard questions, but mix your questioning with sincere submission and seeking of the Lord's will. God wants to use you and your church to make a direct, frontline impact in his worldwide Surge.

That said, I have just one more suggestion: If you are succumbing to the God-given passion to go and make disciples, would you consider going to some of the *least known* of the *least reached* to do something strategically important? Would you allow God to place you (your family and your church) on the tip of his spear, at the forefront of his work?

The opportunity for this is very real: while thousands of unreached people groups have been *identified*, many of them have never been *investigated*. Spend some time today clicking through a few of the people group profiles on JoshuaProject.com, and you will see that the information we have on some of these groups is very limited. Consider the possibility of putting together a short-term project with the sole intention of visiting an unreached people group, praying aggressively for them, and then strategically investigating them so that the information you obtain can be made available to the worldwide church. What if you and your family simply went to look, listen, taste, smell, and feel what life is like for those who have never seen the light of truth or tasted the refreshing water of the gospel?[20]

Roger Peterson of STEM (Short-Term Evangelical Missions) and David Armstrong of Mission Data International and Short TermMissions.com estimate that only one in five short-term mission projects intentionally targets unreached peoples. The rest of our resources are going to communities where there is already a church present. What if we were able to reverse that statistic, and four out of five of the two million Christians who go on short-term mission trips each year went to visit the unreached?

Short-Term to Lifelong

Looking back at that night on the basketball court in the Philippines, I had plenty of time to ponder what I had experienced on my trip. It was a long flight from Manila back to Wisconsin, and I traveled with the constant memory of a small Filipino pastor who was putting his life on the line day after day. After our plane landed, I had a few hours to talk with my parents before I left again on a trip to South America for another tour of duty with Sports Ambassadors.

"If that is what it means to be a pastor, I want to be one," I told my dad. Keep in mind that my father is Stuart Briscoe, one of the great preachers of our day and pastor of a megachurch in Southeastern Wisconsin. Growing up in his home, I had learned firsthand what a life of pastoring, preaching, leading the church, and shepherding God's people was all about — but it wasn't until I met this Filipino pastor that God brought it all together for me in a clear sense of calling.

"Well, Pete, if you have sensed God's calling into ministry, there are two things you need to be aware of," my father said. "First of all, you have severely limited the potential pool of spouses, because you will need to marry a girl who has been called to ministry too." *Dang; hadn't processed that into the decision.* Before I had a chance to reconsider, though, his voice interrupted my musings. "And second," he continued, "if you are going into ministry, you have a choice: you can either be a missionary or a mission-minded pastor. Missions is in the heart of our Savior, and the Great Commission he left with all disciples provides the permeating impetus for the body of Christ. It is what drove the vision of the early church. The reason a lot of churches are dying is because they've forgotten their mission, to make disciples of *all nations*, and have become holy huddles instead." He paused thoughtfully. "We need mission-minded churches, Pete, and this type of church grows only when carefully nurtured by a mission-minded pastor."

If my father's words were true in 1983, I believe they are even more true, and necessary for us to hear, today. With the proliferation of new believers in South America, the persecution of disciples in East Asia, the lack of education of pastors in Africa, and the infiltration of Islam in Europe, the need for mission-minded churches and mission-minded pastors is greater than ever. I was blessed to have been taught this by my father and my professors at school — I knew this truth in my head. But God used a short-term mission trip to get it into my heart, to stir a holy passion for his global movement of love for the nations. Short-term missions have been used by God and will continue to be used by him to change lives that, by his grace, will transform the destiny of entire nations and people groups.

A Church in the Surge
Youth Groups and the Surge

Bent Tree Bible Fellowship
Carrolton, Texas
www.btbf.org

Amy Cedrone, our student missions coordinator, calls it the "Infusion of Compassion." She's not sure where it came from or where it's going, but when she looks at the hearts of the students she works with, she sees it clearly.

"This generation has something innately born into them. They have a keen awareness of the needs in this world, and they want to do something about it. Our responsibility as the older generation is to help them find the opportunities, to equip them, and to give them permission to go out and make a difference. We're no longer trying to give students a passion for missions, because they have that passion. Our challenge is to figure out what that looks like for them."

To facilitate life-changing experiential learning for our students, Amy and her staff have created a multilevel approach that includes, for each age group, an environment for life transformation before, during, and after the short-term project. They aim at specific variables: *responsibility*, *investment*, *intensity*, and *exposure*. Ideally, a student will follow the flow into more intense situations without being overwhelmed.

Level 0: Kindergarten through sixth grade, entry-level missions. Students help with VBS, church services, the food bank, and work at the rescue mission. Sometimes they follow the flow of the donated food from beginning to end — from the excess donated by the grocery stores to the meal prepared for a hungry child.

Level 1: Seventh grade, regional service. Trips take students away from their homes, and the work is a little more intense, requiring greater ownership from those who go. There's more personal devotional time and more time for self-exploration.

Level 2: Eighth and ninth grade, service and wilderness. In addition to level 1 activities, students participate in a leadership development unit in the wilderness. These trips stretch students mentally, physically, and spiritually. The wilderness experience is typically followed by a week of serious mission work.

Level 3: High school, Costa Rica or Honduras. Students go on cross-cultural trips that are workload intensive and require higher levels of personal responsibility and decision making. Kids begin making real decisions that affect the outcome of the trip.

Level 4: High school leadership, international. Students lead teams of their peers, under the oversight of their mentors, on a trip to a foreign country. These trips are completely led by trained and mentored youth. One student is responsible for purchasing the plane tickets, another for arranging the food, a third for setting up the details of the work project, and another for leading the worship and devotions. The adults are along to insure safety, answer questions, and prevent anarchy.

Amy and her teams aren't messing around with the Surge. "We are seeing what God can do through a normal kid. This is the real deal," she says. "Unless we live to see Jesus come back, these will be the leaders of the future, and there's no reason why they can't be the leaders in the service of today."

For those of us adults who are secure enough in Christ and bold enough in our faith, these kids' testimonies speak to our soul as well. They are piercing wake-up calls that can rouse us from our mature slumber.

Chapter 8

Go

When the God Who Sends Lives in Us

Most men are not satisfied with the permanent output of their lives. Nothing can wholly satisfy the life of Christ within his followers except the adaptation of Christ's purpose toward the world he came to redeem. Fame, pleasure and riches are but husks and ashes in contrast with the boundless and abiding joy of working with God for the fulfillment of his eternal plans. The men who are putting everything into Christ's undertaking are getting out of life its sweetest and most priceless rewards.

— J. Campbell White (1909)

A ship in the harbor is safe. But that is not what ships are designed for.

— Unknown

Sitting in my office one afternoon, I was meeting with a young, professional woman who could barely mask the enthusiasm that sparkled from her eyes. "How did someone like you get to this point in your life?" I asked her with a bit of wonder at her situation. She just smiled at me. "I just kept saying yes to the next thing."

Let me explain. "Coleen" had been climbing the corporate ladder, but years ago she had made a decision to follow the Lord, and now, with passport and ticket in hand, she was preparing to leave her successful career to live in an Islamic country and work among an unreached people group.[21] Not long ago, such a move wasn't even on her radar screen. Coleen wasn't sure where her decision to follow Christ would lead her, but she decided that she would faithfully take one step at a time. So she took a step of faith, then the next, and another after that. In making these small choices of obedience, Coleen just kept saying yes to God's plan for her life. She went on a short-term mission trip and was struck by the need of people in a specific part of the world. After returning home, she found that she had been "infected" — not with a tropical disease but with a passion for a certain people group. Now, after following God's lead, she was ready to commit to a long-term investment of her time and energy.

A Sending God

Our God is a sending God. It's not just something he *does*; it's who he is — a part of his nature, a reflection of his character. Throughout Scripture, we see that God *sends*, and he is still sending today! Rather than trying to convince you of this, I'll let God's Word speak for itself:

> *Genesis 12:1:* "The LORD had said to Abram, 'Leave your country, your people and your father's household and go to the land I will show you.'"
>
> *Genesis 45:4 – 8:* "I am your brother Joseph, the one you sold into Egypt! And now, do not be distressed and do not be angry with yourselves for selling me here.... God sent me ahead of you to preserve for you a remnant on earth and to save your lives by a great deliverance. So then, it was not you who sent me here, but God."
>
> *Jeremiah 7:25:* "From the time your forefathers left Egypt until now, day after day, again and again I sent you my servants the prophets."
>
> *Galatians 4:4 – 5:* "When the time had fully come, God sent his Son, born of a woman, born under law, to redeem those under law, that we might receive the full rights of sons."

Luke 4:18 – 19: "The Spirit of the Lord is on me, because he
has anointed me to preach good news to the poor. He
has sent me to proclaim freedom for the prisoners and
recovery of sight for the blind, to release the oppressed, to
proclaim the year of the Lord's favor."

John 6:38 – 39: "I have come down from heaven not to do my
will but to do the will of him who sent me. And this is the
will of him who sent me, that I shall lose none of all that
he has given me, but raise them up at the last day."

John 6:29: "The work of God is this: to believe in the one he
has sent."

In John 6:25 – 57 alone, Jesus alludes ten times to being sent by
the Father! Jesus spoke of a deep conviction that he had been sent
by the Father into the world to save it. This is the ultimate sending,
the one that underlies all others and makes them possible. As long
as there are sheep outside his flock, Jesus will send us. As he has
said, he is the shepherd who leaves the ninety-nine sheep who are
already safe in the fold and goes out to find the one sheep who is
still lost. Jesus is also the master who calls us to walk in his foot-
steps. So are we willing to go where he sends? And are we ready to
become churches that send others?

"How, then, can they call on the one they have not believed
in? And how can they believe in the one of whom they have not
heard? And how can they hear without someone preaching to
them? And how can they preach unless they are sent? As it is written, 'How beautiful are the feet of those who bring good news!'"
(Rom. 10:14 – 15).

Why do we send? We send because our God is a sending God.

Because He Is in Us

As God's children, we have inherited his character and his mission
of sending and going. While it's a mandate — a command — to do
what he asks us to do, it goes much deeper than that. The Surge is

not just a ministry, something we do because God asks us to do it; it's our *identity*. Because God's Spirit now indwells our lives, his passion for the nations *becomes* our passion. That passion may be skewed at times and can be masked by the lies of our flesh and the conditioning of the world, but in every follower of Christ it is there. Wherever the Spirit is present, we will sense God's passion for lost people and his driving desire to save them through the gospel message of his love.

> Repentance and forgiveness of sins will be preached in his name to all nations, beginning at Jerusalem. You are witnesses of these things. I am going to *send* you what my Father has promised; but stay in the city until you have been clothed with power from on high.
>
> — Luke 24:47 – 49, emphasis added

By God's grace, we have been included in the unity that exists between Jesus and the Father (John 17:20 – 21). We share in their oneness and experience unity with other Christians by having a shared purpose and the same passion as our Father. Together, we stand as a single body, dependent on the Spirit to work through us, so that together we can reveal the glory of God to the world. The Surge is not a program or strategic plan that we impose upon our churches. It's not really even something *we* do. The Surge is God's work in and through us, and it begins in our lives with the realization that we are created to be God's children, heirs and descendants of our Father's dream. That's our legacy. God is the source and root of the Surge. His love calls us to know him, and that same love beckons us to join him in his work.

The needs of lost people will call out to those who embrace their identity as children of God — those willing to jump in headfirst, plunging body and soul into the stream of God's love for unreached nations. God sent his Son to save and redeem us, and Jesus willingly went where the Father asked him to go. Now we are being sent — not under obligation or begrudgingly but as a natural consequence of Christ in our lives: "Christ in you, the hope of glory" (Col. 1:27). This is the secret of the Christian life: we say yes to the Spirit of God *in* us, and he does his work *through* us.

Understanding and embracing this truth changes everything. Jesus has promised us that all authority on heaven and earth has been given to him, and as he indwells our lives, that same authority now belongs to us. We know that we will be victorious and will accomplish our mission, because Christ himself is reaching the world through the church. This is about more than just mustering the courage and energy to complete a task; it's about surrendering to become what we already are. I believe this is why we find such tremendous pleasure in being part of the work that God is doing — the sending-and-receiving work of the Surge. The work we do brings harmony and consistency to our being.

When we suppress the call, like I recently did in the Delhi airport, we inevitably feel a great sense of discomfort. My son, Cameron, and I had missed a connecting flight from Delhi to London, and we were waiting in the airport in Delhi for six hours before the next flight would be available. The delay meant that we would also miss our connection in London and would have to spend an additional day sitting in the airport

> Those who are directed to do hard jobs for God must remind themselves that these rigors are simply for their health.... People who regard themselves as invalids rather then heroes will make excellent missionaries.
>
> — Daniel Fuller, *Gospel and Law*

there as well. Needless to say, I was a bit upset, and I uncorked my frustration on the poor guy at the check-in desk (as if it were his fault that the planes weren't on schedule). After letting off some of my anger, I realized what I had done and apologized to him and to my son. I now wonder if that delay, as frustrating as it was at the time, wasn't orchestrated by God in some way. You see, while we were stuck at the airport waiting, Cameron struck up a conversation with Hannah, a young woman from Amsterdam. Traveling home alone after a harrowing experience in Tibet, she latched onto us for the next four hours. She was desperately looking for a safe man, and she found two in us, and of course we were there because God had sent us. We talked, laughed, and played cards ... but never spoke of anything significant. *Jesus, you sent me, and you collided my life with hers, and I didn't think to speak of you ...*

> The call of God does what the call of man can't. It raises the dead. It creates spiritual life. It is like the call of Jesus to Lazarus in the tomb, "Come forth!" (John 11:43). We can waken someone from the sleep with our call, but God's call can summon into being things that are not (Rom. 4:17).
>
> — John Piper, *Desiring God*

I grieve that encounter as a missed opportunity. When God sends us, we need to be prepared to share his love with those we meet.

Jesus made it controversially clear that he was sent by the Father; Jesus also made it clear that he had come to send his disciples as well. We reject his call at great expense and receive it with even greater blessing.

"Jesus went around teaching from village to village. Calling the Twelve to him, he sent them out two by two and gave them authority over evil spirits" (Mark 6:6 – 7).

"As you [Father] sent me [Jesus] into the world, I have sent them into the world" (John 17:18).

You may recall Isaiah's account of his remarkable experience the day he was brought to heaven and given a glimpse of the magnificence of the Holy One. All around him, angelic beings were singing thunderous praises to God, and Isaiah's heart cowered at the revelation of God's holy might: "'Woe to me!' I cried. 'I am ruined! For I am a man of unclean lips, and I live among a people of unclean lips, and my eyes have seen the King, the LORD Almighty'" (Isa. 6:5).

At that point, a seraph flew to Isaiah and touched his lips with a coal and informed him that his guilt had been taken away, that his sins had been atoned for. Isaiah barely had a moment to contemplate his newly forgiven state before God asked him a question: "Then I heard the voice of the Lord saying, 'Whom shall I send? And who will go for us?' And I said, 'Here am I. Send me!'" (Isa. 6:8).

Isaiah was forgiven so that he could be sent. And because he responded to God's call, the course of history was forever changed by the work of the Spirit through this man.

Jumping In

Today thousands of newly formed local churches across the globe are responding to the inner call of God's Spirit to send and go. They are reclaiming this key aspect of their identity, and rather than delegating the responsibility of the Great Commission to mission agencies or relegating the role of "goers" to a few select, trained individuals, these churches are rising up to experience the joy and the challenge of this crucial element of the Surge. Powerful, mobilizing ministries are at work within denominations. Parachurch ministries are partnering with churches and other ministries and sharing hundreds of years of experience and some of the best, cutting-edge resources. Through formal and informal global networks, God is weaving together a plan to see the Great Commission fulfilled.

One such mobilization movement is called TOAG (Training for Ordinary Apprentices to Go).[22] The founder and leader, "Nathan J'Diim," prefers to not have his true name in print, but he's happy to talk about who they are and what God is doing through them as an organization: "TOAG is what she has always been: an experiment, a desperate attempt to equip affluent, institutionally nurtured, comfort- and security-loving Westerners to launch messy, organic Church Planting Movements of quickly reproducing Jesus Communities among unreached, unengaged peoples who inhabit some of the most unwelcoming places on earth."

> We have the DNA of the early church, we have the hope of Christ in us and we go with the expectation that we will win. That's what I long to see birthed in churches today!
>
> — Nathan J'Diim

TOAG's passion is to "envision the local church" to take on a warfare mentality and go to the nations with the aim of seeing entire people groups come to Christ. "We figure that to win, we must unlearn some of the ways of our highly structured, rather expensive, staff intensive, slow-to-reproduce Western-style churches — the only 'church' we have ever known," Nathan says. "We must also relearn the forgotten ways of former days when the early church exploded from 20 thousand to 200 million in just a couple centuries."

TOAG team internships are being organized across North America in key locations with high concentrations of immigrants and international students. For ten months, interns learn by doing as they balance their jobs and family responsibilities with cross-cultural ministry engagement.

TOAG represents a new breed of mobilizers — men and women who combine near-reckless abandon with an overflowing passion for people to know about and experience God's love. The audacity of their God-sized faith makes them willing to have brash expectations: "Our goal is to deliver entire people groups from the kingdom of darkness and usher them into the kingdom of God's beloved Son," says Nathan J'Diim. TOAG is training people to launch rapidly reproducing church planting movements among the unreached peoples. A church planting movement (CPM) is defined as the birth of at least one hundred churches at least three generations deep, showing that the movement is reproducing itself as churches plant churches that plant churches.

Our weary Western hearts and skeptical evangelical minds might be reluctant to aim so high, but we needn't be so cautious. God is unleashing the Surge in full force among the many places around the world where he is transforming entire people groups. Recently Nathan interviewed a number of church planters among the Ansari Muslims of northern India, where 465 house churches have been planted within the last seven years. In Mauritania, West Africa, he saw the in-process birthing of dozens of fellowships among the Pular people group. Heidi Baker and Iris Ministries have seen an explosion of church growth, with 770 simple churches planted among the Makhua Muslims of Mozambique.

I know that unconfirmed reports can be greatly exaggerated and that we must always be careful to verify the accuracy of the numbers we quote. Still, we can verify at least three hundred thousand people coming to Christ out of Muslim backgrounds in Bangladesh. And in the Horn of Africa alone, there are at

> We are convinced that our world needs thousands of Jesus' disciples committed to a passion for Jesus, for his kingdom and to live their lives strategically advancing this kingdom. We must keep experimenting till the DNA flowing through the church in China flows also in our veins, till God can use us to plant millions of Jesus Communities not just in China but among every people on earth.
>
> —Nathan J'Diim

least a half dozen CPMs raging through previously unreached Muslim people groups. One indigenous organization that Nathan recently visited in Africa saw over two hundred thousand Muslims enter the kingdom in just fifty-two months. Such reports are becoming so frequent, it's almost as if the King is preparing to return any day now!

But "Is He Safe"?

Imagine Moses, standing barefoot and bewildered before an ignited bush that refuses to burn up. Suddenly an unexpected message radiates from within, becoming audible to his ears: "The cry of the Israelites has reached me, and I have seen the way the Egyptians are oppressing them. So now, go. I am sending you to Pharaoh to bring my people the Israelites out of Egypt" (Exod. 3:9–10).

If I were Moses, my first thought would be, *Why would God send someone he* loved *to the very place he had fled from?* After all, could there be a more dangerous place for a renegade Israelite than the courts of Pharaoh? Why would God choose to put such a burden on the shoulders of any man (unless of course we're talking about Chuck Norris or Charlton Heston)? God tells us why he chooses to send Moses. He sends him, he says, because *"the cry of the Israelites has reached me."* This interchange reveals one of the great paradoxes of the Surge: God is committed to reaching those who are far from him, *and* he is willing and ready to send his loved ones into harm's way to reach the lost with his love.

Let there be no doubt. One of the primary values of contemporary Western evangelicalism is *physical safety*. Likely, you are familiar with the popular cliché that has been circulated among us, playing off our desire to be safe, comfortable, and secure: "There is no safer place than in the center of God's will." *Really?* Is following God's will the *safest* place to be? Tell that to Jesus while he hangs on a cross; tell that to Paul as he pulls the seaweed out of his ear and nurses the snakebite on his hand; tell that to the disciples as they find themselves exiled from their loved ones or hanging upside down on a cross because they refuse to deny their faith in Christ. For that matter, try sharing that bit of wisdom with Martin Luther or John Wycliffe. Far from being a *safe* place,

I would argue that the center of God's will is, for many of us, an extremely *dangerous* place to be.[23]

I have had numerous conversations with representatives and leaders of mission organizations bemoaning the fact that they often find young people eager to be sent, only to learn that their parents have nixed the idea or strongly discouraged it. The reason these parents give? "It just isn't safe anymore." Anymore? When was it *ever* safe to follow God, to share the gospel, to witness to God's love in a foreign land? And why do we insist on elevating our safety, as if being safe and secure were of greater importance than obeying God? Throughout the Scriptures, we see that God didn't hesitate to send people, regardless of the potential danger. When we are sent, we join a long line of spiritual ancestors who lived (and died) while faithfully following Christ.

Far from encouraging his followers to stay safe, Christ invited them to *die* when he asked them to pick up their crosses and follow him. It's really not a question of *if* we are going to die; it's a matter of *when* and *for what cause*. The Surge gives us an eternal cause that is not only worth living for but also worth dying for. It's a cause that has motivated countless men and women, over thousands of years, to sacrifice their lives in service to the King of Kings.

> I'm convinced that we are living in what appears to be the most cruel period in history. More people suffer for Christ's name than in any other generation.... We should not expect something easy. We should pursue what is worthy, whatever the cost.
>
> — Brother Andrew, *God's Smuggler*

That said, we must also be careful that we do not misrepresent the nature of the cause we serve, just to recruit people to join us. Is the Surge an adventure? Certainly. A privilege? Absolutely. An essential expression of our true identity? Naturally. But it is also a *war*. And like any war, it requires blood, sweat, and sacrifice.

Following Jesus has *never* been safe. This illusion of security is a luxury limited to modern Christians living in the affluent Western church. The Surge is not always safe. But it's certainly worth the cost, even at the cost of our physical security.

Catch and Release

Robert Lewis, a pastor and church leader I admire, recently did something very courageous: still in his fifties — the prime of his ministry years — he stepped out of his role as the senior pastor of Fellowship Church in Little Rock, Arkansas, and handed the reins to a younger guy. Lewis is now investing his life in discipling men and mentoring young leaders. I became the beneficiary of his decision recently at a Leadership Network event I attended.

Robert described to us a survey conducted by Fellowship Little Rock in the mid-nineties. The church asked their members to indicate how long they had been attending and then to rate their satisfaction with Fellowship. The survey showed that during the first, second, and third year of attending the church, the satisfaction level was very high. But then, after year four, the satisfaction level began to decline. By year seven, there was a high level of dissatisfaction among the church members.

> While I applaud the student movement, I think it will help when the church congregation sees itself as the seed bed or breeding ground for potential missionaries.
> — Gordon MacDonald

As Robert and his team studied the survey results, they discovered two important characteristics of those who had indicated the highest level of dissatisfaction: they tended to be *more* mature spiritually (defined by participation in a regular practice of spiritual disciplines), and they were *less* engaged outside the walls of the church than the more satisfied groups.[24] These findings were seminal in guiding Fellowship toward becoming an outwardly focused church. While I was listening to Robert speak, pondering the implications of all this for our church, my thoughts were interrupted by his closing statement: "Christianity is not a catch-and-keep proposition; it is catch-and-release."

For those of you who aren't sure what Robert Lewis was saying, my guess is that you aren't all that familiar with fishing lingo. Let me help you understand. There are essentially two ways to fish: (1) you can catch a fish and keep it (a common strategy among many churches fishing for men and women), or (2) you can catch a fish and then release it, sending it back out into the environment from which it came. Our responsibility as a church body is to be fishers of people (Matt. 4:19), sharing the good news about Jesus with them, discipling them, helping them discover their spiritual gifts, and teaching them what it means to be transformed by the Spirit. We catch, but then we must also learn to *release*, sending people back out into the environment from which they came. That last step is not an optional calling for a select few churches or parachurch organizations. It is a biblical imperative, necessary for the ongoing life and health of the church — and for those we catch up into our churches.

I went fishing recently with a good friend, Mike, on his Texas ranch. God's grace was freely upon us that day, and we hauled in thirty-five black bass by the time the sun was setting in the western sky. We had intended to catch and release, moving the larger fish to a different lake and throwing the smaller ones back so they could grow into trophy fish. Our dry well on the boat was filling up with lots of mature fish, while their smaller kin were joyfully swimming away after being released from the hook. As the sun started to set, the fish just kept biting, Mike and I started talking, and … well, let's just say that we forgot about the fish in the dry well for a while. Suddenly remembering, Mike jumped up and flipped open the lid. To my horror, I saw the bulging underbellies of the five large fish we had caught and kept that day. "We've got to get them back in the water right now!" Mike yelled. As we raced to throw them back in the lake, I couldn't help but compare the way the two types of fish would reenter the water. The smaller ones would gleefully swim off with energy, passion, and blazing speed. The larger ones drifted off slowly and in some cases remained upside down for several minutes. By keeping the fish in our well too long, we had almost killed them.

I hope the analogy is clear: Some of the people we "catch" will be released back into the water around our boat, others will be transferred to waters in other parts of the world, but we've still got to get them in the water somewhere, and if we wait too long … well, we risk creating "belly-up believers." Those who are released into the Surge, however, will dive and thrive — and likely survive the wounds of battles fought outside the "safety" of the boat. You'd be amazed at some of the bite marks we find on fish we catch! God calls us, as individuals and as a church, to be *in* the world but not *of* it. We are *sent* into the world (John 17), but without a firm grasp of our essential identity as senders and goers, we inevitably become *of* the world *in* the church, bickering about temporal earthly concerns, stagnating and slowing dying in the "safety" of our churches.

The Master Fisherman was very clear about the best way to help a fish survive: "Whoever wants to save his life will lose it, but whoever loses his life for me and for the gospel will save it" (Mark 8:35). We can try to play it safe inside the walls of our churches, or we can lose our lives in the Surge and actually save them by serving God. As disciples of Jesus Christ, we are both fishermen — always carrying the hook of the gospel with us, ready to share — and fish, swimming out to the wide open seas on the Surge of God's love for the world.

Sending is now one of the core values at Bent Tree: "We send out missionaries, we send our kids on short-term trips, we send our church family into the world each week to be salt and light as Jesus lives his life through them. Our gathering times are also equipping times, so that we can be encouraged, taught, and trained to go back into the world and influence our unique sphere of influence. Our goal is not to grow a big crowd but to develop an impassioned body of disciples who view themselves as sent to a desperate world in need of Christ."

The Surging Legacy

Our missions pastor, JoAnn Hummel, was recently visiting with leaders of the underground church in China and was amazed to witness the burgeoning drive of these persecuted believers to take the gospel back to Jerusalem. They reassured her and urged her not to worry about reaching the Islamic world with the gospel; they were confident that Christ was going to use China to win large numbers of Muslims to Christ (reminding her that manpower was not a problem for them in China!). Manpower is no longer a concern for the international church of the twenty-first century.

Our brothers and sisters around the world understand and embrace the sending character of God and are eager to walk in obedience to the Great Commission. What they are lacking, in many cases, are resources:

> The surprising fact is that Mongolia tops the list as the most efficient missionaries-sending country. One out of every 222 Mongolian believers service with a mission organization.
>
> — Jason Mandryk, *Perspectives on the World Christian Movement*

money, experience and expertise, training for pastors, and material needs like shoes, motorcycles, food, and Bibles.

One immediate consequence of the surging growth of the worldwide church is that the resource base to further the remaining work of the Surge is rapidly growing. Believe me, I know that on this side of the ocean, it doesn't always seem like much is happening, but it's quite true! From a personnel standpoint alone, we have more committed Christians (and a much higher ratio of Christians to non-Christians) than ever before in world history.

Practicing Christians as a Percentage of Total World Population since 1900

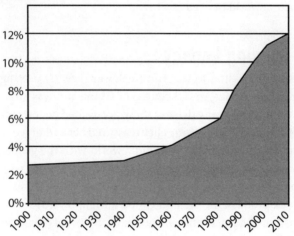

It took eighteen centuries for practicing Christians to grow from 0 percent of the world's population to 2.5 percent in 1900, only seventy years to grow from 2.5 percent to 5 percent in 1970, and just forty years to grow from 5 percent to 12 percent by the year 2010. Today there is one practicing Christian for every seven people worldwide who are either nominally Christian or non-Christian.

Ralph D. Winter and Bruce A. Koch, "Finishing the Task," in Ralph D. Winter and Stephen C. Hawthorne, eds., *Perspectives on the World Christian Movement* (Pasadena, Calif.: William Carey Library), 531.

The Diminishing Task

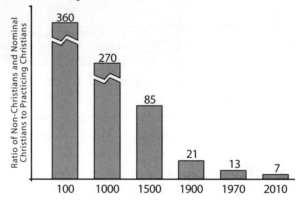

Ralph D. Winter and Bruce A. Koch, "Finishing the Task," in Ralph D. Winter and Stephen C. Hawthorne, eds., *Perspectives on the World Christian Movement* (Pasadena, Calif.: William Carey Library), 544.

While the stats can (and should) encourage us, the task of reaching the world can still seem overwhelming, impractical, and even impossible. *And it should!* Our mission and purpose as a church, and our witness to the world, is not simply to do a pretty good job of accomplishing reasonable things in our own strength. We must not grow overly confident in ourselves or in our accumulated resources, as if the Surge of God's redeeming love were simply a matter of

> God never asks us to do anything we can do. He asks us to live a life which we can never live and to do a work which we can never do. Yet, by his grace, we are living it and doing it. The life we live is the life of Christ lived in the power of God, and the work we do is the work of Christ carried on through us by his Spirit whom we obey.
>
> — Watchman Nee

sufficient manpower. No, our sufficiency is in Christ alone, not in our own methods or resources. Instead may we be known as churches that pushed the edges of faith, dreamed God-sized dreams, counted our lives as loss in order to gain Christ, and went out to the nations with a passion inspired by nothing less than the passion of God himself!

The Prayer of Our High Priest

The silhouette of the cross loomed just over the horizon. Within hours, Jesus would willingly be arrested, rejected by the Jews, beaten, and killed. Intentionally and solemnly, he prepared himself to endure the cross. For the joy set before him, he set his face toward Golgotha — but not before lifting his eyes up to his Father and making petition for his bewildered and conflicted ragtag band of followers: "My prayer is not that you take them out of the world but that you protect them from the evil one. They are not of the world, even as I am not of it. Sanctify them by the truth; your word is truth. As you sent me into the world, I have sent them into the world" (John 17:15 – 18).

Then, amazingly, the prayer request of Jesus moved beyond his disciples standing before him and crossed the ages, as he lifted up prayers for the spiritual generations yet to come — a prayer spanning two millennia: "My prayer is not for them [the disciples] alone. I pray also for those who will believe in me through their message [you and me!], that all of them may be one, Father, just as you are in me and I am in you. May they also be in us so that the world may believe that you have sent me.... I in them and you in me. May they be brought to complete unity to let the world know that you sent me and have loved them even as you have loved me" (John 17:20 – 23).

I have just one simple question for you to consider right now. Are you willing to ponder the implications of Jesus' prayer for you? Will you take a moment to stop and listen to the prayer of *your* High Priest, spoken for *you* hours before his crucifixion, now echoing through time toward its future fulfillment? Do you sense your Lord's prayer being answered in you ... right now?

"How beautiful on the mountains are the feet of those who bring good news, who proclaim peace, who bring good tidings, who proclaim salvation, who say to Zion, 'Your God reigns!' ... Depart, depart, go out from there!" (Isa. 52:7, 11).

The Surge continues! Stay up-to-date with the latest statistics, and celebrate verified accounts of recent church planting movements at *www.GetInThe Surge.com.*

A Church in the Surge
An Extra-Ordinary Church

Faith Church of the Valley
Chandler, Arizona
www.faithchurchaz.org

If you happen to drive by Faith Church in Chandler, a suburb of Phoenix, Arizona, you will likely not bother to give it a second glance. Step inside the church on a Sunday morning, and you'll probably feel right at home rubbing shoulders with evangelical brothers and sisters, sharing hot coffee and donuts in the foyer, as in thousands of churches all over the country. But take another step into the sanctuary, and things might start to look a little different. National flags representing some of the most difficult to reach and spiritually needy countries hang from the ceiling, and photo montages of church planting teams hang on the walls. *Hmmm, something is happening here.* The pastoral staff at Faith Church has been ministering together for over three decades. And while the church offers the full range of family-focused ministries, underlying everything they do is a mature and ever-evolving passion to see Christ glorified among all peoples. Under the surface of this "ordinary" church is a body of believers who have gotten caught up in the Surge.

"When we started, it was all about church-based teams," says senior pastor John Salvatore. "We wanted to send teams from our body that were fully supported by us, and we continued doing this for more than a decade. But the idea caught on *too* strongly. Our missions-mobilizing pastor drips with passion; he efficiently trains and recruits people to be sent out, but our vision eventually outstripped our financial resources. We just couldn't sustain multiple teams from within our body indefinitely."

Having reached a crossroads, Faith Church began networking with other like-minded churches, offering to train and equip their people. "It's even gone beyond that; we are training churches to train *other churches* to train *teams* that strategically plan to start church planting *movements*," says Salvatore. "'Planting' has to do with addition; 'movements' have to do with multiplication, but that requires innovation, simplicity, and a radically different approach to 'church' than we have been accustomed to."

Along the way, a fair number of mistakes have been made, and difficulties and struggles are the norm, both on the field and at home. Team unity is always difficult. Culture shock, spiritual warfare, strong personalities — everything is multiplied on the field. The first team the church sent came apart on the field. One of their strongest missionaries died, leaving a wife and three daughters to continue the work. Associates of another team have been martyred. The church has people in harm's way in numerous war-torn global hotspots. One woman almost died of an illness contracted on the field. And since the church is targeting some of the hardest-to-reach people among the unreached, they constantly have to keep their expectations in check.

"God will reach these peoples on his own time frame," Salvatore says. "But we send people out with the understanding that they might be just moving the rocks for the first ten years — just clearing the field so that the soil can be tilled. After that, hard soil must be broken up before seeds can be planted and they start to grow."

Faith Church's long-term commitment to reaching the nations means that they are now sending "kids" who caught their world vision in the church's elementary and junior high programs. One of those "kids" is leading a team of medical missionaries working with nomads in one of the most difficult to reach areas of the Middle East.

"We want to invest in churches that share God's passion for the nations and are doing something about it. We don't have unlimited time, but we are ready to partner with churches who adopt this sending vision and are ready to go for it. As other churches catch the vision, we can greatly multiply our efforts on the field."

Chapter 9

Yes

When Adopted People Adopt-a-People

> God is pursuing with omnipotent passion a worldwide purpose of gathering joyful worshipers for himself from every tribe and tongue and people and nation. He has an inexhaustible enthusiasm for the supremacy of his name among the nations. Therefore, let us bring our affections into line with his, and, for the sake of his name, let us renounce the quest for worldly comforts and join his global purpose.
>
> — *John Piper, Let the Nations Be Glad!*

The technical term is *infanticide*. It's similar to the word *insecticide* (a chemical to get rid of unwanted pests) and the word *herbicide* (a spray to get rid of weeds). Unfortunately, *infanticide* doesn't refer to getting rid of bugs *or* weeds. It's exactly what it sounds like.

Recently the reality of infanticide became quite personal for me. I was spending some time with a missionary family living in India whom we support, the Mennons. They mentioned that in Indian culture, male babies have value, but in some areas of the country, female babies are considered a liability — excess luggage. So the families just discard them, like trash tossed away on the side of the road.

Literally.

Several years ago, the Mennons learned about a newborn baby girl who had been left on the side of the road. There was no need for them to "give it some time and pray about it." They had the Word of God in their heart, they heard the still, small voice in their spirits, and they knew there was only one choice to make. They rushed over and picked up the girl from where she had been left. *Only two days old* — but still alive. They took her back to their home, nursed her back to health, and held her in their arms ... and then in their hearts. *Yes,* they knew, *this one is ours.*

Word quickly spread throughout their community. The next time a girl was found among the trash, someone went and told them. And the next time. And the next. Now they have twenty-two little girls and counting, all rescued within the first year of their lives. These girls are all safe now, living in a home with warm beds and food on the table, embraced by an uncommon family that bursts at the seams with laughter and love. The first group of girls to be saved is now in school, learning what it means to be a Christ follower, and growing up to be leaders in the Indian church.

The Mennon family portrait is a beautiful picture — a living mural proclaiming the identity transformation that lies at the heart of the gospel, the beautiful truth of our adoption.

Photo courtesy of Mike Neukum

A Different Kind of Spirit

I have two amazing nieces. (I actually have more than two, and they are all amazing, but I'm focusing on just two of my amazing nieces as I write this.) They belong to Dave and Sarah (my wife, Libby's, sister and her husband), who added these two dark-skinned, multicultural children to their fair-headed family about fifteen years ago, rescuing them from a life of need and struggle. I have to confess that I love the looks I get when we are out in public together. Everyone who sees us tries to figure out who belongs to whom. But the truth isn't very complicated: they belong to our family in the same way that we belong to the Father, by adoption. "For all who are being led by the Spirit of God, these are sons of God. For you have not received a spirit of slavery leading to fear again, but you have received a spirit of adoption as sons by which we cry out, 'Abba! Father!' The Spirit Himself testifies with our spirit that we are children of God, and if children, heirs also, heirs of God and fellow heirs with Christ, if indeed we suffer with Him so that we may also be glorified with Him" (Rom. 8:14 – 17 NASB).

Adoption is not just an analogy or symbol of our salvation in Christ; it is a true reality for those who put their faith in Jesus. Our adoption is a certificate of guarantee by our heavenly Father that we belong to someone who will never forsake us or reject us. Each of us was born into sinful flesh, lived as a resident of the kingdom of darkness, and was left abandoned by the side of the road, at the mercy of an evil world — until Jesus found us, took our sins as his own, made us new creations, and filled our new hearts with the very presence of his life-giving Spirit. Now we live as residents of the kingdom of light, children of the King of Kings. The spirit of adoption flows in our veins. It reminds us where we have come from and who we have become, *and it defines what we naturally do.*

I can't think of a better example of the truth of our adoption than Alan Hunt. Not many years ago, Alan would have been near the top of the "least likely to do something extreme for Christ" list. In his previous life, he sold auto parts, investing thirty-two years as a national account manager for a Fortune 500 company. He had grown up in the church and racked up years of perfect Sunday school attendance, but looking back, he feels like it was all just a good front. When the Hunts started coming to Bent Tree, however, Alan said yes and began attending our "Top Gun" men's Bible study. Under the caring mentorship of other men, and habitually renewing his mind with the truth of Scripture, he began to realize his new identity as an adopted son of God.

A gradual transformation took place in his life. Alan soon discovered that he had the gift of evangelism, and he said yes to being trained through Evangelism Explosion, eventually saying yes to becoming an EE trainer and then to leading a forty-person team with the Need Him call centers. Soon he found himself smuggling Bibles and gospel tracts into Cuba, taking the Perspectives class on the worldwide missions movement, and being mentored through our REACH training ministry. All this was leading up to the day when he had the physical sensation that God was lifting him out of his position in the corporate world and planting him in the world of orphans. God's adoption of Alan was about to come full circle.

Alan now serves as vice president of Church Partnerships and Advocacy for World Orphans *(www.worldorphans.org)*. "My job is to recruit, train, lead, and work with a variety of people and churches. World Orphans is a global ministry that works exclusively through Western and indigenous churches," he says. Where his life used to be consumed by quarterly sales figures and strategies, the Spirit in him now drives him to fulfill a different purpose: "World Orphans is committed to rescuing millions of orphaned and abandoned children, the strengthening of thousands of indigenous churches, and the impacting of hundreds of communities with the gospel of Jesus Christ ... through the cost-effective empowerment of church-based orphan prevention, rescue, care, and transition programs in the least reached areas of the world."

Alan took a leap of faith, right into the Surge, and is in all the way over his head — and he knows it. He now finds himself frequently traveling internationally and constantly walking by faith, but he discovers time and time again that God is directing his steps. Two years ago, for example, he found himself in Rwanda, an African country of ten million that has been devastated by genocide, HIV/AIDS, and extreme poverty. This has resulted in an estimated eight hundred thousand orphans. Next to a closed and dilapidated school on a local hilltop, he and a Rwandan pastor named Enoch prayed for homes for orphans and a Western church partner who would provide some sustainability for the construction of new homes and renovation of the school. In faith, the construction began.

Not long after that, Alan was standing beside his display booth in the exhibit hall at a large church conference in California. He recalls, "Two young ladies approached, and one introduced herself as Rachel, a pastor's wife from Northpointe Community Church, a small fellowship in Johnson City, Tennessee. Her husband had sent her to the conference to find a ministry their church could partner with to engage in orphan care. She boldly stated, 'I have talked with every ministry in this exhibit hall, and y'all are it!' After a moment of speechlessness, I said, 'Awesome!' The woman with her, Amanda, then told me that they really have a heart for Rwanda. 'Y'all have any projects there?' Of course we'all did."

Please understand. This isn't a megachurch partnership. Northpointe consists of a website *(www.northpointejc.com)*, some donated office space, and about one hundred people who meet each week in a school gymnasium. They had no illusions about their ability to contribute financial resources, so their effort began on their knees with friends from several churches in the area. From these prayer meetings, three couples from three separate churches joined together to form a group called HOPE 2.2.1. (It stands for: two countries, two histories, one future.)

HOPE 2.2.1. formed a short-term team that traveled with Alan on a vision trip and visited Pastor Enoch's church/home/school project on the Rwandan hill. With little hesitation, the Tennessee team said, "Yes. These children and this project are ours." They committed to a partnership and began planning the next steps almost immediately. Upon their return home, a "Night for Rwanda" dinner

> When we were children, we were in slavery under the basic principles of the world. But when the time had fully come, God sent his Son, born of a woman, born under law, to redeem those under law, that we might receive the full rights of sons. Because you are sons, God sent the Spirit of his Son into our hearts, the Spirit who calls out, "*Abba*, Father." So you are no longer a slave, but a son; and since you are a son, God has made you also an heir.
>
> — Galatians 4:3 – 7

was held, and over 140 people from a variety of local churches attended. The HOPE 2.2.1 vision was taking shape.

"Today there are twenty children between the ages of two and nine living in two homes," Alan says. "All are double orphans, and three of them are HIV/AIDS positive. The school is operating again, with a new roof and remodeled classrooms. The partnership continues to grow and evolve. New relationships have been built in the community through medical, sports, and community outreach events. Planning is underway for the next short-term team trip focusing on a clean water project and developing a biosand filter microbusiness to provide sustainability income for the project."

This is the way God works in the Surge as leaders network together for innovative ministry: a car parts salesman, a pastor and his abandoned building in Africa, and a small Tennessee fellowship with a heart of willing compassion — all captured by the spirit of adoption. Working together, they are turning their experience of spiritual adoption in Christ into a powerful witness of God's love through the physical care of orphans.

The Question

Adoption agencies have learned that it is necessary to take ideas and concepts and personalize them to help people grasp them and connect with the children behind the idea of adoption. They do this every month through magazines, radio, and television, and they are good at it! From all around the world, they bring us pictures, stories, and descriptions of children. They know that if you look into the eyes of these precious kids and then look into your own heart, something inside will inevitably prompt the question, *Is this one ours?*

I wholeheartedly support the ministry of orphan care and believe it is an essential element of God's purpose in the Surge. But I want to push you to think further, beyond the particulars of orphan and adoption ministries, to ask a related question. What if, just as potential parents look into the eyes of *orphans*, our local churches looked into the eyes of *the nations* and asked that same question: *Is this one ours?* What if every church made a commitment to adopt a people group as if it were their own child: praying for the people, strategizing how to reach them with the love of Christ, networking with other ministries, and endeavoring with all their strength to see that unreached nation come to know Jesus?

Agencies like World Orphans aren't afraid to pull on your heartstrings. Don't mistake the resulting sensation for false guilt or oppressive obligation. These ministries simply know that we are motivated to action when ideas are personalized. They know that if they can get you to look long enough, you'll see that "the question" is not rhetorical or hypothetical. These are

> We want to accept personal responsibility for reaching some of the Earth's unreached, especially from among the billions at the widest end of the gap who can only be reached through major new efforts by God's people. Among every people group where there is no vital, evangelizing Christian community there should be one, there must be one, there shall be one.
>
> — David Bryant, *In the Gap*

real children, *real* people, and *real* choices between life and death. If you're convinced that a baby is not in your future, I suggest not opening the magazine from the adoption agency! Seriously, these things should have labels on them that say, "Warning: The contents of this document might convince you to do something outside your comfort zone, push you to the edge financially, and totally mess up your plans for retirement and an empty nest." No, if you like your life as it is, if you and your church are comfortable being comfortable and content being content, then you should probably put this book down right now and do your best to quiet the spirit of adoption that might already be whispering to your soul.

For the rest of you, however, I would like you to consider yet another option. Regardless of whether God is calling you to adopt a *physical* child and bring him or her into your family, we need to understand and *personalize* God's passion for the spiritually orphaned nations of the world — the eight thousand remaining people groups of the world who lie on the sides of the religious roads of the world. We know *who* they are and *where* they are. Ethnographers and missiologists have located them, cataloged them, and packaged their photos for us to see. Would you dare to open the "magazine of the nations" and take a look in the eyes of these precious future children of God, waiting to be adopted into his family? Do you dare to ask the question, *Is this one ours?*

Snapshot of the Nations

The remaining eight thousand unreached people groups can be divided into five major religious blocks with the approximate numbers:[25]

    Muslims (3,300)
    Nonreligious (100)
    Adherents of Ethnic Religions (1,200)
    Buddhists (700)
    Hindus (2,400)

Numbers are just numbers; behind each of these figures are real people, real needs, and real opportunities. Let me introduce you to just a few of these "children" waiting to be adopted into the family of God.

Muslims: The Herki of "Kurdistan"

For unknown centuries, the Herki people lived as nomads, wandering season after season across the mountains of central Asia with their herds and families. Today they fight for individual survival — as well as for a national identity — never giving up the dream that they might someday have a land under their own name. For the time being, they live in a place called "Kurdistan," in the mountainous area where the borders of Turkey, Iran, and Iraq meet. Hated by the Iraqis and shunned by the Iranians, they have found themselves caught in the midst of various wars and conflicts between these nations. In addition, they have been fiercely engaged in a bloody and stalemated civil war with the Turks, and they have no one to support them or fight alongside them. Even among their fellow Kurds, the Herki find themselves divided and isolated, cut off from help.

Courtesy of the International Mission Board of the SBC. Used with permission.

The Herki look to the religion of Islam and a militant social order for justice. They are Shafite Sunnis, descendants of an earlier faith that was pagan and violent, setting them apart from other Muslims. In the rural areas, some of the Herki people still believe that spirits can take on human or animal forms.

Several mission agencies are targeting the Herki, but very little progress has been made. Neither the Bible nor Christian radio broadcasts are available in the Herki language. Wars, tribal unrest, and decades-old suspicion of Westerners exponentially complicate efforts to reach them.

But nothing is impossible for God; there are Herki people who are called to belong to his family. What if a local church were to adopt the Herki and start by mobilizing an ongoing prayer blitz for them? Would we begin to see some of their bondage and isolation softened through the spiritual requests of committed intercessors?

Nonreligious: The Han Chinese

The Han are the largest people group in the world, totaling somewhere around 1.3 billion people. Yes, you read that right — 1.3 *billion*. Most Han live in mainland China, but the Han have been fleeing to other countries since the Mongol invasion of 1276, dispersing across the globe, driven from their ancestral homeland by centuries of political, military, and economic conflict. The Han tend to congregate in urban areas, often forming their own little "Chinatowns."

Today the Han can be found in diverse nations all across the globe: fifty thousand Han live in Italy, forty thousand in Cuba, one hundred and fifty thousand in Australia,

Courtesy of the International Mission Board of the SBC. Used with permission.

and one hundred thousand in Saudi Arabia! In countries such as Laos, Nepal, Tanzania, Cambodia, and Thailand, the Han have yet to be reached with the gospel.

Stop and imagine for a moment: what if individual churches around the world adopted the Han that have come to their own cities and began to strategically minister to them?

Adherents of Ethnic Religions: The Ashéninka of Peru

Mysterious, tribal, and animistic — the thirteen thousand Ahé-ninka are the stereotypical "heathen tribe" of decades past. Little is known about them except that they share a common language and a definable territory. They speak South Ucayali, an indigenous American language spoken along Perú's Upper Ucayali River. Who are these people? What are their needs? We really don't know yet.

So much remains to be discovered about this unknown and unreached group of people. What if an adventurous college Sunday school class chose to adopt them and then headed down to Peru for a spring break mission trip, to pray

Courtesy of the International Mission Board of the SBC. Used with permission.

on location for these people and take some initial steps to learn more about their culture and their needs as a people?

Buddhists: The Khmer of the United States

In April 1975, the Cambodian government fell to the Communist Khmer Rouge. Masses fled the country by any means possible in an effort to avoid the horrific onslaught of the Killing Fields, where thousands were murdered. The Khmer people living in the United States number about two hundred thousand. Though 4

Courtesy of the International Mission Board of the SBC. Used with permission.

percent of them claim a Christian affiliation, researchers estimate that only about 0.5 percent (five out of one thousand individuals) are Bible-believing followers of Jesus. Strong Khmer churches can occasionally be found in America, but the rest of these people practice Theravada Buddhism seasoned with ancestor worship and animism. Many Khmer people drop out of high school and few ever attend college, leaving the Khmer at the bottom of the socioeconomic scale for immigrants.

Could a local American church begin a new work with the Khmer, possibly equipping and mobilizing a local Khmer church in an effort to further reach the thirteen million Buddhist Khmer still living in Cambodia (which is 0.5 percent Christian)?

Hindus: The Mahratta

In the western-central regions of India you'll find the Mahratta, a heaving mass of humanity nearly fifty million strong! Clothed in vibrant colors, individuals are easily lost in the swell of this vast ocean of people. The Mahratta are one of the largest unreached people groups on earth.

Courtesy of the International Mission Board of the SBC. Used with permission.

Highly spiritual, they seek the power and approval of the gods. Some look toward black magic for guidance; almost all believe that the cow is sacred. They gather at their temples to pray, and daily seek the guidance and favor of any number of the 330 million Hindu gods.

Just think what could happen if a church were to join forces with Mahratta Christian leaders by offering resources and training to mobilize them to reach their own nation? This is not a hypothetical question! In fact, that was the very question I asked myself in 2003 when less than *two hundred* Mahratta were following Christ. As a church family, we stopped in the midst of our busy lives, looked the Mahratta people in the eye, and asked ourselves: *Is this one for us? Should we adopt this people group as our own?*

Six years later . . .

Fast-forward to 2009. I was sitting in a small office in Pune, India, sharing tea with the leaders of a group of church planters I had come to know as my brothers. (Pune, if you haven't heard of it before, is an "average-sized" Indian city — about seven million people.) Almost sixty months had passed since Bent Tree first joined forces with the International Leadership Academy and the Maharashtra Leadership Academy, a platoon of Indian believers committed to training and developing pastors and evangelists to reach out to the Mahratta nation by sending church planters to unchurched areas and starting church planting movements. The news that day was very positive: Thirty-three church planters had started ninety-one cell groups attended by 835 Mahratta! Ten churches had been planted, and 399 people were attending worship services. Turning to me, these leaders asked if the vision had changed or if they should keep moving ahead on the course we had chosen to pursue five years ago.

I paused. Bent Tree's dream for the Mahratta people is that every one of them would have access to a gathering that lifts up the name and person of Jesus. *Dozens of cell groups; hundreds of worshipers?* It was all encouraging, but I was still reeling from the day before, when I had traveled through the streets of Pune to a large dam on the outskirts of the city to "see the water" (a favorite Sunday afternoon pastime). The two-lane streets were crammed with cars six wide; motorcycles with entire families aboard skittered in and out; pedestrians filled any leftover gaps in this creeping glacier of color, cars, and people. After four hours of sitting there, I asked Sashi, one of the church planters, who was perched in the front seat, "What percentage of these people we have seen today know Jesus?" "I would be surprised," he replied, "if one percent do." As I pondered the masses outside our vehicle, the enormity of the need in this place washed over me like a tsunami. *It's David verses Goliath . . . multiplied by fifty million.*

Should we keep moving ahead on the course we had chosen? The immensity of the task overwhelmed my limping heart as if I were a climber contemplating Mt. Everest. I thought, *Sure, let's keep the mission the same, and ... good luck with* THAT! Fortunately, that isn't what came out of my mouth. I am convinced that God's Spirit spoke through me to encourage the leaders in that office when I said to them, "The vision remains unchanged. Let's see every person in this state have access to a life-giving church! Bent Tree is up for it if you are, but let's adjust the time frame a bit. Jesus is free to move up our time frame if he wants, but we are in this for the long haul. Friends, we may not see this dream become a reality in our lifetime, and neither may our children, but I am convinced that our grandchildren will. This not a ten-year project — this could take one hundred years. And I just want to tell you that it is a great joy for me to sit in a room with the grandparents of this movement!"

Destiny and Reality

The Mahratta are just one patch in the quilt of the nations, one tile in the mosaic of the unreached peoples of the earth. Will there one day be groups of Jesus worshipers among this hardened and yet beautiful nation of forty-seven million people? Impossible as it might seem at the moment, the answer is an unequivocal yes! How can I answer you with such resolute certainty?

First and foremost, God's Word promises me that it *will* happen. "Who will not fear you, O Lord, and bring glory to your name? For you alone are holy. All nations will come and worship before you, for your righteous acts have been revealed" (Rev. 15:4). The day *will* come when the gospel of God's kingdom will be preached as a witness to all the nations. This is not an obscure theological idea but a prophecy that is becoming a reality before our very eyes. The Surge is not a means without an end. It's not a philosophical vision that lacks a plan or a goal. We are not just treading water. The Surge flows with powerful currents in the direction of the fulfillment of Matthew 28:19 and Matthew 24:14. You may have a hard time believing that God is fulfilling prophecy as you sit and read this — and I don't blame you if you do! I think one of the curses of living in a relatively stagnant spiritual society is that we've become accustomed to the status quo and are ignorant of the massive movement taking place all around us on a global scale. The fulfillment of the Great Commission to disciple the nations is not an if. One day God *will* receive the worship due his name among the Mahratta people. We have his Word on that, and God is always true to his Word.

Second, from a merely human perspective, the "chances" of the Mahratta people group being reached are better now than ever before in history. We've looked at graph after graph that visually depicts the Surge that we are experiencing across the globe. None of the graphs we have seen, however, show the potential for reaching the unreached nations better than this one:

The Growth of Churches to Peoples

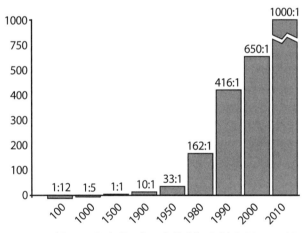

Ralph D. Winter and Bruce A. Koch, "Finishing the Task," in Ralph D. Winter and Stephen C. Hawthorne, eds., *Perspectives on the World Christian Movement* (Pasadena, Calif.: William Carey Library), 545.

For just a moment, I need you to seriously contemplate what these rising bars mean. If you are still unconvinced that God has the resources to finish the task of reaching the world with the gospel, then this should convince you. Take note: There are *one hundred times* more churches per people group now than there were in 1900. There are *thirty times* more churches than there were in 1950, and over *twice* the number that there were in 1990, and we are beginning to head off the charts. In other words, there is an exponential multiplication taking place. New churches are not just the *fruit* of the Surge; they are its *fuel* as well. Not only are there more churches, but also the churches that exist today are more evenly spread throughout the nations. This is a movement that has been developing over the last century, and now a major shift has become verifiable.

Dinesh D'Souza communicates some of these trends in his book *What's So Great about Christianity?* and he begins with a quote from Philip Jenkins' book *The Next Christendom*: "The era of Western Christianity has passed within our lifetimes, and the day of Southern Christianity is dawning." D'Souza continues, "The vital centers of Christianity today are no longer Geneva, Rome, Paris, or London. They are Buenos Aires, Manila, Kinshasa, and Addis Ababa."[26] Statistics now prove the truth of this shift with staggering clarity. "In 1900, more than 80 percent of Christians lived in Europe and America. Today 60 percent live in the developing world. More than two of three evangelical Christians now live in Asia, Africa and South America."[27] According to further research by Jenkins, Europe today has 560 million Christians and America has 260 million, yet most of these are *nominal* Christians (in name only). In comparison, there are 480 million Christians in South America, 313 million in Asia, and 360 million in Africa. The vast majority of these are *practicing* Christians. His conclusion: Third World Christianity is coming our way. South Korea has become the world's second-largest source of Christian missionaries. Only the United States sends more missionaries to other countries,[28] and South Korea is only one-sixth our population!

Geographic, linguistic, and cultural barriers still exist that insulate each unreached people group from the gospel, but because of this shift in evangelical demographics, many unreached nations are "closer" culturally and geographically than ever before ... *and* we have an unprecedented force of churches to reach out to them ... *and* we are doing it:

In 1986, Nigerians were sending slightly more than 500 missionaries; in 2006, that number had increased to 5,200. Brazil was sending 595 in 1972; in 2000 they were sending 4,754. In 1979, Korea was sending 93; now there are 16,000 serving in 168 countries. The India Missions Association was started in 1977 with five members. Today they are sending more than 50,000 through 220 organizations.[29] The Surge is now an unrestrained global movement, flowing in all directions at once. And with over one thousand churches for every unreached people group on earth, don't tell me God hasn't given us the human resources to accomplish what he has commanded. We lack *nothing* — except possibly the willingness to say yes!

> We need one another. The church in the non-Western world owes much to the prayers and labors of the Western world. We wouldn't be here otherwise.... non-Western missions movements are equal and able partners. I believe the convergence of these two great missions movements will result in a powerful end-time harvest machine!
>
> — Bernan Kumar, executive director of Strategic Missions Partnerships

Steps to Yes

Across the globe, we are witnessing a strategic outpouring of people and resources through local churches as they network with the worldwide body of Christ to finish the task and ride the Surge to its fulfillment. Part of the strategy taken by many of the churches is the "adopt a people group" concept. Don't be overwhelmed by stats and numbers. Start by reminding yourself that this is God's work and not ours. Without him we can do nothing, yet all things are possible through him.

Second, know that you don't have to reinvent the wheel. You just need to find the wheels that best fit your church. Small or large, each local fellowship plays their part in this work. We need only do what God is already wanting to do through us. No more, no less. Many churches take that first frightening step of faith only to find that God already has a work prepared for them; all they need to do is walk in it (Eph. 2:10).

The process of adoption, as you might imagine, involves several elements, but these can come together in any order. You might already be well on your way toward adopting an unreached people!

1. *Pray!* Give the idea back to God. Ask for a willing heart and clear direction. Pray for the nations and the people groups that are unreached. Several agencies have really good resources for this.[30] The next time you are in Colorado Springs, stop at the World Prayer Center at New Life Church, where you can join believers on their knees 24/7/365 as they pray for the nations.

2. *Explore!* Ask God to give you his eyes to see the world as he does, then start looking around. Look in your own backyard, at your local university, and at local cultural centers. Surf www.JoshuaProject.net, or better yet, get the latest copy of *Operation World*. Once you have a potential nation in your sights, see if you can visit the people of that nation face-to-face.

Prayer/research expeditions, where you visit the people group you have adopted, are one of the most valuable short-term investments you can make, allowing you to contribute the information you collect to the mission databases. Prayers never come back unanswered, and you may be the first person to ever pray for these places and faces! God often spontaneously uses these research/prayer teams to touch and transform lives along the way.

Explore the strengths and weaknesses of your church. Are there already natural connections or relationships with an unreached people group? Do you have a people group very near you geographically? What are your worldly passions? Do you have hobbies, skills, or vocational abilities that will equip you to reach one people group more effectively than another? Consider how God may already be at work in your church, and look for connections and opportunities you may have never noticed before.

3. *Network!* Those who have adopted children know that there are some great and wonderful resources available to help you through the process. The same is true for adopting a people group — check out one of the many "people group adoption agencies" available to help you in your search. A particular mission organization may already be devoted to reaching your specific nation. Your denomination may already have a unique focus on a certain corner of the world. A sister church within your denomination may be willing to share your passion if you approach them with the possibility of working together. It's also likely that you can network with other churches and parachurch organizations (see the Adopt-a-People Clearinghouse at *www.adoptapeople.com*). You might even find a group already on the ground, working to reach your unreached people!

4. *Decide!* Once you are sure you know which people group God is burdening your heart for, be sure to register your intentions at the Adopt-a-People Clearinghouse *(www.adoptapeople.com)* so others can find you for networking and sharing of resources.

5. *Go for it!* Pray, listen, watch ... God will show you the way forward. Dream your dreams and plan your ways, knowing that God will direct your steps (Prov. 16:9), but you must take that first step; that first yes must come from your lips. There is no need to rush, but don't put this off for too long. Remember, unreached people groups lie out there like abandoned spiritual infants left on the roadside.[31] Would you dare to look them in the face and ask yourself, "Is this one ours?"

A Church in the Surge
Adopting the "You"

Crossroads Christian Church
Vacaville, California
www.vvcrossroads.org

When George Ripley came on board as the worship pastor at Crossroads Christian Church in Vacaville, California, he was initially skeptical. Along with a number of tyrannically "urgent" responsibilities, he had inherited a former leader's fading vision: reaching the people group we'll simply call the "You."[32]

In 1995, the missions team at Crossroads began looking for ways to strengthen and expand the existing missions vision of their congregation. Hoping to move beyond their "Jerusalem and Judea" focus, they sought to discover the joy of following Jesus to the ends of the earth, and they found it by adopting a people group. The missions team began by educating themselves, sharing with each other what they were learning in Sunday school classes and small groups. Several people took the Perspectives class, offered through an extension in their town by the U.S. Center for World Mission. The church took out a bulk subscription to *Mission Frontiers* magazine. Then, at one of the meetings, while praying through the monthly prayer guides from the Joshua Project, they began to sense that they were supposed to focus their passion on a nation they code-named the "You." God's providential hand began to lead them forward. "Chance meetings" and "accidental networks" began showing up, all pointing them in the same direction.

Crossroads was the first church to call the You their own. At the time they said yes, the You had no Bibles, no radio, no literature, nothing to tell them about God's love for them. For several years, the vision was sustained by a handful of faithful people on the missions team ... until those members moved from the church. When George came on board as a new pastor, he and the remaining team members had to ask themselves a difficult question: *Are we* still *committed?*

"The emphasis on this one group was costly and consuming. I wasn't sure it was worth it," George confesses. "Then I went to a conference in Canada where multiple churches were meeting for a semiannual conference on this people group. What I saw and what I heard resolidified our decision. After years of hard work, we were starting to see a wave of impact headed our way. *We don't want to get off now!* I thought."

Crossroads is now an integral part of a growing network of churches and ministries who have adopted this group. As a church, they have supported missionaries through YWAM, helped develop a radio program through Trans World Radio, and participated in Bible translation work through RUN Ministries.

"God is at work among this group. This is not the time to give up hope. We saw the wave coming; now we are starting to ride it. It's a tough thing sometimes. You hang in there and stay determined and committed. Anything difficult that you work at, no matter what it is, makes success all the sweeter. A lot of tears have been shed for these people, but this is the lifeblood of the church — something *we* need as well as them."

This last summer, all the churches that have adopted the You gathered for a weekend conference in Denver. The progress is exciting. Conservative estimates are that over five hundred You are now committed followers of Jesus. George found out firsthand, however, that this isn't just a statistic.

"Several You came to the conference this year. They shared amazing testimonies about how the gospel came to them and how their nation is being reached. It's one thing to look at the numbers, but it's something else to see them and meet them and look into their eyes. That makes it real. That makes it worth it."

People Group Adoption Certificate

Believing Father God has adopted us into his kingdom, and Jesus has purchased people from every tribe, language, people, and nation by his precious blood shed on the cross (Rev. 5:9), and Christ has commanded us to preach the gospel to the ends of the earth (Acts 1:8), making disciples of all nations (Matt. 28:18 – 20), and the people of our culture have ready access to the gospel and there are still millions of people in the world with no such access, and God has led

to do our part in helping a specific unreached people group worship his Son, Jesus (Acts 16:6 – 10; Ps. 67), we hereby adopt the

(people group), pledging ourselves from this day forward to pray regularly for the establishment of an indigenous, reproducing church among them, and to continue to do so until our prayers are answered. In addition, we proclaim ourselves willing to be led by God into further involvement in the task of reaching this people group in any or all of the following ways:

- Working to raise consciousness of their need within our congregation
- Giving of our time, treasure, and talent to work among them
- Sending people to work among them, both short-term and long-term
- Partnering with others who have these same adoption goals

By signing this, I covenant to diligently seek God's will for my life, family, and church in regard to this adoption of the

_____ ,

and to solemnly undertake to fulfill all these stated responsibilities and others inherent in this act of adoption as they are revealed to us by God.

Signed: _____

Date: _____

Adapted from the original Crossroads Christian Church certificate.

CONSUMED
Surging toward Eternity

> Then the angel showed me the river of the water of life, as clear as crystal, flowing from the throne of God and of the Lamb down the middle of the great street of the city. On each side of the river stood the tree of life.... And the leaves of the tree are for the healing of the nations.
>
> — *Revelation 22:1 – 2*

Malcolm Hunter is a great speaker, but he should come with a warning label: "Caution! One-on-one conversations with this man could prove to threaten your current lifestyle!" Malcolm has served Christ for decades in some of the bleakest conditions imaginable in the heart of Africa, and that night, my wife, Libby, and I were driving him through north Dallas to our church building to speak at our annual mission festival. It takes approximately seven minutes to drive from our home to the church building, and in that short time we passed no less than seven churches — one of which boasts a membership somewhere north of twenty thousand people. We made pleasant small talk for most of the drive before Malcolm asked me the obvious but unspoken question.

"Why are you here?" he asked.

"What do you mean?" I asked.

"I mean, why are you living and serving in *Dallas*? This city is already saturated with good churches and great preachers. So why are you here? Come with me to Addis Ababa, Ethiopia. There is an expatriate church there composed of some of the most influential leaders in all of East Africa. They *need* a pastor. This city doesn't need you; let's get you in the right spot."

Libby and I had been serving at Bent Tree for about five years when Malcolm dropped this bombshell on our heads. The best response I could muster at the time was the familiar evangelical delay tactic, "I'll pray about it." This time, however, the question didn't just fade with time. Another defining moment had caught up with me, and I knew in my heart that I couldn't shrug it off. For several sleepless nights his question tormented me, opening the door to deeper introspection, soul-searching, and conversation with God.

Lord, why did you call us here? Why are you keeping us here? What do you have in mind for us here? Is it time to start packing?

Tony Campolo once accused Christendom of avoiding the authentic, hard questions. He asserted that we have learned to ask only questions we already have answers to — the questions we *want* answers to — and that we dodge inquiry into domains that could threaten our status quo and reveal the flimsy barriers of our comfort zone. I'll admit, life in the proverbial spiritual desert of Western Christianity is not always pleasant, but it seems relatively safe to us. It is known and familiar. It is comfortably uncomfortable, predictable, and seemingly secure. We often avoid the hard questions that have the potential to lead us to a new place, the questions that challenge us to dive headfirst into the Surge.

That's why guys like Malcolm are truly dangerous: they don't know (or don't care) which questions are permissible to ask in the church and which are not. Worse yet, people like Malcolm have often taken great steps of faith in their own life and now have this uncomfortable habit of seeing the possible in the obviously impossible. Not only do they think the unthinkable (like upending everything to relocate in the forbidden corners of the planet); they have done it. Now looking back from the other side, they see no problem with inviting us to step across the threshold to join them on an adventure beyond the grey curbs of suburbia.

I pray that as you've read this book, you have been challenged and provoked to face the difficult questions with honesty, faith, and humility:

- What am I to be about? What am I *really* supposed to be doing?
- Who am I? Who am I *really*?
- And what about these people with whom I share the journey, this thing called church? Who are these people that I lead? Who are these people that I follow? Who are those who walk beside me as my friends, comrades, and partners in this peculiar faith? ... And to what have we been called, *really*?

Together, verse by verse, story after story, we have seen what happens when churches and individuals catch the wave of Christ's love for the nations. The answers to most of our questions aren't usually found in carefully planned strategies and programs. They are found when we take a step of faith and dive into the raging movement of our Savior's love as it spreads throughout the world. It's a movement that is flowing toward the fulfillment God's purpose for his creation, propelled by the wave of the Spirit toward the final consummation: an ocean of redemption for all eternity, for all peoples.

We have investigated and shown you how

- the deluge of God's swelling passion and the flood of his Spirit are being poured out on this world *today*;
- the central theme of "the nations," from Genesis to Revelation, is what shapes and defines for the church a clear, biblical measurement for success, and how God is unquestionably successful in his endeavors thus far to reach the world with the gospel;
- God's passion for each of us, as individual leaders, is an indispensable prerequisite for authentic Christian leadership.

As seasons come and go, and as I travel to more and more corners of the globe, I am increasingly convinced that Christ is the hope of a dying, desperate, and deluded world. Because the church carries with her the life, love, and message of Christ, the church delivers that hope. We have now entered a time when Christ, through the church, is rapidly closing the gap on the fulfillment of Matthew 24:14 and Matthew 28:19. The Surge is a verifiable, intentional, and inevitable movement of God's Spirit, and according to nearly every major indicator, it *is* happening right now.

> The church is the most magnificent concept ever created. It has survived persistent abuse, horrifying persecution and widespread neglect, yet it is still God's chosen instrument of blessing. It is the greatest force on the face of the earth. Local churches, large or small, can do incredible things. Churches working together in networks can do even more.
>
> — Rick Warren

The explosive potential of "virtual missions" is only beginning to be realized. The nations have arrived on our doorstep, and modern transportation has made the world more accessible, putting the entire globe within a day's reach and increasing the possibilities for well-conceived short-term mission projects. Now that the task that remains has been made clear and measurable, we can send out people with precision and wisdom. And we can witness, in a practical way, to our own adoption as children of God by taking steps to adopt unreached people groups as our own, nurturing their spiritual development through prayer and strategic vision trips.

Modern tools and technological innovations are being mobilized to communicate a timeless truth: we have been crucified with the risen Christ. The great mystery and the great truth we confess is that we no longer live for ourselves, but Christ is living through us in all that we do and say. Without him we can do nothing, but through him all things are possible.

The question Malcolm asked me that night in our car is a question we each need to ask ourselves: "Why am I here?"

God, why did you call us here? Why are you keeping us here? What do you have in mind for us here? . . . Or is it time to start packing?

All of my questioning and contemplating led me to one conclusion and two options. First, I concluded that getting caught up in the Surge wasn't optional. Missions isn't a program of the church; it's the lifeblood of our calling and our ministry. To deny myself and my church members the joy of getting caught up in this dramatic and unprecedented outpouring of God's love for the nations would be to deny our very identity as a church: who God has made me and my church to be. In light of this inescapable conclusion, I could see only two options: either I needed to do exactly what Malcolm was asking me to do — leave it all behind and become a missionary in Africa — or I could dedicate my life to mobilizing incredible yet dormant resources of the Western church as a mission-minded pastor.

Where . . . how do you want to live this out through me, Lord? In the mosaic of the worldwide church, which tile am I?

One evening, while badgering God with questions, I sensed his answer for me. His still, small voice whispered to my spirit, *I have you here so I can grow a church of mission-minded disciples through you, and then I am going to use that church to touch the world.*

The Lord made it obvious to me that he could leverage my gifts for the world church much more effectively in Dallas than if I were to go to the mission field myself. I am convinced that this is a primary reason why any pastor is placed in the Western church today — to mobilize our local churches to resource the world church toward the ongoing fulfillment of the Great Commission. Certainly, our congregations must continue to focus on the six key purposes of the church — spiritual growth, worship, community, evangelism, service and mission — and I wholeheartedly believe that a pastor's role is to grow the church along these lines. But I am also quite certain that there resides in the Western church a unique responsibility to steward the financial and human resources of her people toward the goal of reaching the nations for Christ.

That was my answer when asked years ago, and it continues to be God's call upon my life as I serve Bent Tree today. Tomorrow? Only God knows what role each of us will be playing as the drama of the ages unfolds in this fragile and fluid sliver of history. Some of us will be sent; others will do the sending. Some will reach the world as it comes to our neighborhoods; others will find the nations online. Many will serve behind the scenes, using their unique skills to support and mobilize others, and each of us will find freedom and joy as we discover, time and time again, how Christ wants to love the nations through us.

> Missions is not the ultimate goal of the church. Worship is. Missions exists because worship doesn't.
> — John Piper, *Let the Nations Be Glad!*

Surging toward the Eternal Consummation

Looking at the current state of Western Christianity, our emotions and experiences would likely tell us that the American church is playing defense and the worldwide movement of Christ has grown stagnant. But the facts prove us wrong. When we can measure that over two-thirds of all the reached people groups have been reached in the last thirty-five or so years, and that approximately eight million local churches around the globe can and *are* being mobilized to reach the remaining eight thousand unreached groups, we have good evidence that we are truly standing on the threshold of the final movement of redemption.

How and when this might all take place has been and will continue to be a matter of great debate, of course (making fools of many who have claimed to know the day and hour). And though it may continue to be a question of when, let me encourage you that it is certainly not a question of if. The Surge cannot be suppressed. God is on the move among the nations, redeeming, restoring, and renewing what is rightly his. Famines, earthquakes, and battles are yet to come, but the war is being won. A new dawn is glowing red on the horizon — a day coming when all creation and all peoples will stand side by side singing in perfect harmony, in pure, unhindered, universal song to the omnipotent, loving, and just King of kings and Lord of lords.

It is the coming realization of the vision given to John on Patmos: "Then I saw a Lamb, looking as if it had been slain, standing in the center of the throne, encircled by the four living creatures and the elders.... The four living creatures and the twenty-four elders fell down before the Lamb.... And they sang a new song: 'You are worthy to take the scroll and to open its seals, *because you were slain, and with your blood you purchased men for God from every tribe and language and people and nation.* You have made them to be a kingdom and priests to serve our God, and they will reign on the earth'" (Rev. 5:6 – 10, emphasis added).

It is the coming celebration prophesied in Matthew 24 and described in Revelation 7: "After this I looked and there before me was *a great multitude that no one could count, from every nation, tribe, people and language, standing before the throne and in front of the Lamb.* They were wearing white robes and were holding palm branches in their hands. And they cried out in a loud voice: 'Salvation belongs to our God, who sits on the throne, and to the Lamb.' All the angels were standing around the throne and around the elders and the four living creatures. They fell down on their faces before the throne and worshiped God, saying: 'Amen! Praise and glory and wisdom and thanks and honor and power and strength be to our God for ever and ever. Amen!'" (vv. 9 – 12, emphasis added).

This then, is the very heart of the Surge! It's the one and only appropriate response of the created toward the Creator: pure, mass *worship*! The uprising of praise is growing across the globe and swelling with the overflowing passion of the Father, Son, and Spirit as they fulfill all that has been promised.

Will you and your congregation join in the song today?

For the good of your soul and the strength of your local church, I'm inviting you to submerge yourself in the rushing waters of God's global passion. I'm challenging you to stop right where you are, wherever you are, and listen — listen for the distant thunder of life-giving rivers. Start walking toward a new horizon where the rumble becomes a deafening roar, where the blast of cool mist engulfs you as you ponder the raging current of God's infinite, eternal passion for his people, from every nation, tribe, and tongue … and his deep, abiding love for you.

> Worship, therefore, is the fuel and the goal of missions. It's the goal of missions because in missions we simply aim to bring the nations into the white-hot enjoyment of God's glory.... Worship is also the fuel of missions ... you can't command what you don't cherish. Missionaries will never call out, "Let the nations *be glad!*" who cannot say from the heart "*I rejoice* in the Lord...." Missions begins and ends with worship.
>
> — John Piper, *Let the Nations Be Glad!*

A flood of the power of God's Spirit *is* raining down on this world. A tsunami of praise *is* rising up across the globe, a prelude to the perfection that is being restored. So what about you? Why are you here? The Surge is ready for you. Are you ready to dive in?

"May the peoples praise you, O God; may all the peoples praise you. May the nations be glad and sing for joy, for you rule the peoples justly and guide the nations of the earth. May the peoples praise you, O God; may all the peoples praise you. Then the land will yield its harvest, and God, our God, will bless us. God will bless us, and all the ends of the earth will fear him" (Ps. 67:3 – 7).

NOTES

1. David Kinnaman, *Unchristian: What a New Generation Really Thinks about Christianity ... and Why It Matters* (Grand Rapids, Mich.: Baker, 2007), 25.
2. Jacob Neusner, "Money-Changers in the Temple: The Mishnah's Explanation," *NTS* 35 (1989).
3. Paul wrote in 1 Corinthians 3:16, "Don't you know that you yourselves are God's temple and that God's Spirit lives in you?" In this verse, the word *you* is plural. Paul is speaking of the local body of believers as the temple of the living God. In 1 Corinthians 6:19, the word *you* is singular, speaking of individual believers: "Do you not know that your body is a temple of the Holy Spirit, who is in you, whom you have received from God? You are not your own ..."
4. Depending on how a people group is defined, the numbers will vary, usually between eight thousand and twenty-four thousand people groups. The higher number comes from using the "unimax" definition of a people group, which is most specific in defining barriers of language, culture, and caste.
5. Ralph D. Winter and Bruce A. Koch, "Finishing the Task," in Ralph D. Winter and Stephen C. Hawthorne, eds., *Perspectives on the World Christian Movement*, 4th ed. (Pasadena, Calif.: William Carey Library, 2009), 532.
6. Mark Driscoll, *Confessions of a Reformission Rev.: Hard Lessons from an Emerging Missional Church* (Grand Rapids, Mich.: Zondervan, 2006), 18 – 19.
7. Walt Wilson, "The Transition of Everything from Atoms to Bits," *Lausanne World Pulse*, November 2008, *www.lausanneworldpulse.com/perspectives.php/1043* (accessed July 2010).
8. Sites like womentodaymagazine.com and SecretsofSuccess.com do this as well.
9. Wilson, "The Transition of Everything," 68.
10. Winter and Hawthorne, *Perspectives on the World Christian Movement*, 751.
11. John Ronsvalle and Sylvia Ronsvalle, *The State of Church Giving through 2004: Will We Will?* 16th ed. (Champaign, Ill.: Empty Tomb, 2006), 36.
12. Ron Blue with Jodie Berndt, *Generous Giving: Finding Contentment through Giving* (Grand Rapids, Mich.: Zondervan, 1997), 201.
13. This report is based upon telephone interviews conducted by the Barna

Group, with a random sample of 1,005 adults selected from across the continental United States, ages eighteen and older, in August 2008 *(www.barnagroup.com)*.

14. G. Jeffrey MacDonald, "Rise of Sunshine Samaritans: On a Mission or a Holiday?" *Christian Science Monitor* (May 25, 2006), *www.csmonitor. com/2006/0525/p01s01-ussc.html* (accessed July 2010).

15. JoAnn Van Engen, "The Cost of Short-Term Missions," *Catapult Magazine*, November 18, 2005, *www.catapultmagazine.com/global-eyes/ article/cost-of-short-term-missions* (accessed January 2008).

16. Ibid.

17. Ibid.

18. Terence D. Linhart, "Planting Seeds: The Curricular Hope of Short-Term Mission Experiences in Youth Ministry," *Christian Education Journal*, ser. 3, vol. 2, no. 2 (2005): 266.

19. Tony Campolo, quoted in Paul Borthwick, *Youth and Missions: Expanding Your Students World View* (Wheaton, Ill.: Victor, 1988).

20. As radical as this might sound, it's been done by church after church, dozens of times. A book titled *Exploring the Land: Discovering Ways for Unreached Peoples to Follow Christ* by Shane Bennet and Kim Felder (with Steve Hawthorn) gives ideas about how you can do just that. It is available through Pioneers.org (which offers top-notch resources and advice for anyone who gets caught up in the Surge). And what you learn can be shared with the world's mission force simply by posting it on JoshuaProject.com.

21. For security reasons, we have not disclosed her real name or location.

22. Learn more about this ministry at *www.toag.net* or by calling 602-717-8449.

23. I understand that the intention of some who use this phrase is to point out that our understanding of safety is different than the biblical perspective (and they would agree with what I am saying), but in common use I find that most people think of this phrase in relation to their own personal safety and comfort.

24. The *Reveal* survey commissioned by Willow Creek has discovered similar findings.

25. Remember, these numbers are changing continually! For the most up-to-date numbers, go to *www.JoshuaProject.net*.

26. Dinesh D'Souza, *What's So Great about Christianity* (Washington, D.C.: Regnery, 2007), 7.

27. Ibid., 7.

28. Ibid., 8–9.

29. Winter and Hawthorne, *Perspectives on the World Christian Movement*, 71–73.

30. Start with globalprayerdigest.org, prayway.com, JoshuaProject.net.
31. The Adopt-a-People Campaign has a helpful packet of information on adopting an unreached people group. It's part of the U.S. Center for World Mission, which is also home to dozens of mission organizations. U.S. Center for World Mission, 1605 Elizabeth St., Pasadena, CA 91104, 818-398-2200, aap.campaign@uscwm.org, *www.uscwm.org*.
32. For security purposes, we have replaced the actual name of the adopted people group.

About the Leadership Network Innovation Series

Since 1984, Leadership Network has fostered church innovation and growth by diligently pursuing its far-reaching mission statement: *To identify high-capacity Christian leaders, to connect them with other leaders, and to help them multiply their impact.*

While specific techniques may vary as the church faces new opportunities and challenges, Leadership Network consistently focuses on bringing together entrepreneurial leaders who are pursuing similar ministry initiatives. The resulting peer-to-peer interaction, dialogue, and collaboration—often across denominational lines—helps these leaders better refine their individual strategies and accelerate their own innovations.

To further enhance this process, Leadership Network develops and distributes highly targeted ministry tools and resources, including books, DVDs and videotapes, special reports, e-publications, and free downloads.

Launched in 2006, the Leadership Network Innovation Series presents case studies and insights from leading practitioners and pioneering churches that are successfully navigating the ever-changing streams of spiritual renewal in modern society. Each book offers real stories, about real leaders, in real churches, doing real ministry. Readers gain honest and thorough analyses, transferable principles, and clear guidance on how to put proven ideas to work in their individual settings.

With the assistance of Leadership Network—and the Leadership Network Innovation Series—today's Christian leaders are energized, equipped, inspired, and enabled to multiply their own dynamic kingdom-building initiatives. And the pace of innovative ministry is growing as never before.

For additional information on the mission or activities of Leadership Network, please contact:

LEADERSHIP NETWORK®
innovation series

800-765-5323
www.leadnet.org
client.care@leadnet.org

Leadership Network Innovation Series

Real Stories.
Innovative Ideas.
Transferable
Truths.

How can you fulfill your calling as a pastor or church leader and help your church experience vitality? Learn from those who have gone before you.

Launched in 2006, the Leadership Network Innovation Series presents case studies and insights from leading practitioners and pioneering churches that are successfully navigating the ever-changing streams of spiritual renewal in modern society. Each book offers *real* stories about *real* leaders in *real* churches doing *real* ministry.

The Big Idea
Dave Ferguson, Jon Ferguson & Eric Bramlett

Confessions of a Reformission Rev.
Mark Driscoll

Dangerous Church
John Bishop

Deliberate Simplicity
Dave Browning

Ethnic Blends
Mark DeYmaz & Harry Li

Leadership from the Inside Out
Kevin Harney

The Monkey and the Fish
Dave Gibbons

The Multi-Site Church Revolution
Geoff Surratt, Greg Ligon & Warren Bird

A Multi-Site Church Roadtrip
Geoff Surratt, Greg Ligon & Warren Bird

Servolution
Dino Rizzo

Sticky Church
Larry Osborne

The Surge
Pete Briscoe with Todd Hillard

With the assistance of Leadership Network — and the Leadership Network Innovation Series — today's Christian leaders are energized, equipped, inspired, and enabled to multiply their own dynamic kingdom-building initiatives. And the pace of innovative ministry is growing as never before.

Learn more at www.InnovationSeries.com

Dangerous Church

Risking Everything to Reach Everyone

John Bishop

Dangerous churches are willing to put everything on the line for the one thing that matters most: reaching lost people. Through probing questions and amazing stories of God's grace, John Bishop challenges church leaders to embrace what matters most to the heart of God, whatever the cost.

Most churches gravitate to what is safe and familiar. Church leaders who take risks are bound to fail, and fear drives us to continue in our comfortable but ineffective patterns.

But reaching out to a lost world was never meant to be easy.

Jesus promised his followers that they would have trouble in this world. Dangerous churches are churches that are willing to risk everything—comfort, safety, and the security of the familiar—for the sake of the one thing that matters most: reaching out to people who may spend eternity separated from the God who created them.

God wants us to live on the edge of our margins, walking by faith and not simply following scripted methods or programed patterns. *Dangerous Church* takes us back to the book of Acts and reminds us that the heartbeat of the church is found not in agendas or human plans but in pursuing the mission of God and reaching out to a lost world. Learn what can happen when church leaders abandon their fears and begin to live a dangerous faith.

Dangerous Church is part of the Leadership Network Innovation Series.

The flood of God's passion for the world continues...

www.GetInTheSurge.com

- Blogs by cutting-edge experts
- "Think-tank" forums for sharing strategy
- Recent statistics
- Spirited discussion on controversial topics
- Fresh accounts of Church Planting Movements
- Free resources for small groups and committees
- Sermon recordings with outlines and PowerPoint support
- Links to some of the most innovative churches and organizations on the globe

Ride the wave of Christ's love for the nations.

The Surge is on.

Get in it.

Stay in it.

"Look at the nations and watch—and be utterly amazed."
- Habakkuk 1:5